FRANK LLOYD WRIGHT'S $10,000 HOME

HISTORY, DESIGN, AND RESTORATION OF THE BACH HOUSE

ROBERT J. HARTNETT

HILTON PUBLISHING
Chicago, Illinois

MASTER WINGS PUBLISHING
Chicago, Illinois

HILTON
PUBLISHING

Hilton Publishing Company
5261-A Fountain Drive
Crown Point, Indiana 46307
219-922-4868
www.hiltonpub.com

MASTER WINGS
PUBLISHING

Master Wings Publishing
104 S. Michigan Avenue, Suite 500
Chicago, Illinois 60603
312-374-9455
www.masterwingspublishing.com

ISBN 978-0-9983282-9-4

Angela Vennemann, Senior Editor and Design, Hilton Publishing
Judine O'Shea, Publisher, Hilton Publishing
Megan Lippert, Executive Vice President, Hilton Publishing

Map by Gemma Pauwels, © Master Wings Publishing

Library of Congress Cataloging-In-Publication Data

Names: Hartnett, Bob, author.
Title: Frank Lloyd Wright's $10,000 home : history, design, and restoration of the Bach House / Bob Hartnett.
Other titles: Frank Lloyd Wright's ten thousand dollar home
Description: Chicago, Illinois : Hilton Publishing, 2019.
Identifiers: LCCN 2019013110 | ISBN 9780998328294 (pbk.)
Subjects: LCSH: Emil Bach House (Chicago, Ill.) | Wright, Frank Lloyd, 1867-1959. | Prairie school (Architecture)--Illinois--Chicago. | Chicago (Ill.)--Buildings, structures, etc.
Classification: LCC NA7511.4.C6 H37 2019 | DDC 728/.370977311--dc23
LC record available at https://lccn.loc.gov/2019013110

Frank Lloyd Wright's
BACH HOUSE
N
W. JARVIS AVE.
LAKE MICHIGAN
N. SHERIDAN RD.
W. TOUHY AVE.
LOYOLA PARK
ROGERS PARK, CHICAGO

Client

1333 N. Broadway
Santa Ana, Calif.
Nov. 15, 1956.

Dear Mr. Wright:

This note to you is to serve two purposes: First, it is to congratulate you on your gifts to the world in your architecture style + marvelous plans + ambition to lead people to appreciate the beauty expressed in unusual things.

The second reason is personal. Perhaps you do not remember the little "Dream House" you built for Mr. + Mrs Emil Bach at 7415 Sheridan Rd. Chicago in 1914, but we never forgot you or your wonderful kindness + patience with us at that time. Mr. Bach passed away on March 6th of this year but we often re-lived in memory the happy years we lived in that home until we sold it in 1935. I recall with a thrill of joy the simple beauty of design of the furniture you built, the unusual lighting, the conveniences incorporated,

2

saving of space + above all the "feel" of the black walnut wood used through out the place. Yes indeed it was not only a "livable house" but a "lovable home", thanks to you!

I wish you good health + God's richest blessings.

Sincerely yours
Mrs. Emil Bach

Above/right: a letter from Anna Bach to Frank Lloyd Wright

Below: Wright's response

See opposite page for transcription

Client

Mrs. Emil Bach
1333 North Broadway
Santa Ana
California

Dear Mrs. Bach: Will never forget the "Bach House" nor the Bachs. Glad you remember it all.

Sincerely,

Frank Lloyd Wright

January 21st, 1957

1333 N. Broadway
Santa Ana, Calif.
Nov. 15, 1956

Dear Mr. Wright,

This note to you is to serve two purposes: First, it is to congratulate you on your gifts to the world in your architectural style and marvelous plans and ambition to lead people to appreciate the beauty expressed in unusual things.

The second reason is personal. Perhaps you do not remember the little "Dream House" you built for Mr. and Mrs. Emil Bach at 7415 Sheridan Rd., Chicago in 1914, but we never forgot you or your wonderful kindness and patience with us at that time. Mr. Bach passed away on March 6th of this year but we often re-lived in memory the happy years we lived in that home until we sold it in 1935. I recall with a thrill of joy the simple beauty of design of the furniture you built, the unusual lighting, the conveniences incorporated, saving of space and above all the "feel" of the black walnut wood used throughout the place. Yes indeed it was not only a "livable house" but a "lovable home," thanks to you.

I wish you good health and God's richest blessings.

Sincerely yours,
Mrs. Emil Bach

Dear Mrs. Bach: Will never forget the "Bach House" nor the Bachs. Glad you remember it all.

Sincerely,
Frank Lloyd Wright

January 21, 1957

I dedicate this book to

my wife, Lin,

my son and daughter-in-law and the boys:
Matt, Megan, Henry, and Patrick, and

my daughter, Aimee.

I'd like to thank the following individuals and organizations for their support and assistance, because without their help this book could not have been written:

The Owen Bach Family

TAWANI Enterprises, Inc.

Harboe Architects

The Frank Lloyd Wright Trust

Contents

Foreword

I originally became exposed to Frank Lloyd Wright and the role of architecture in communities when I was a child. We lived in Oberlin, Ohio, for five years, from 1953 to 1958, and my father ran a company in nearby Elyria. While there, we lived next door to the Weltzheimer family, who commissioned their house directly from Frank Lloyd Wright in the late 1940s. We knew the Weltzheimers and I often played with their daughter, Chrissie, who was a bit older than me.

The Weltzheimers retained the house until Margaret Weltzheimer passed in 1963. Private developers then bought the property and made some significant—damaging—alterations. But thankfully, 1968 saw prominent art historian Ellen H. Johnson purchasing the house and overseeing restoration efforts. When she died in 1992, she gifted the house to Oberlin College to serve as a guesthouse and an open attraction for the Art Department and the Allen Memorial Art Museum. My mother and one of my sisters took classes at Oberlin, so the college—and the house— always remained part of my life and on my mind.

I saw how the preservation and love that went into this property translated to a direct and even scholastic asset for the community. With dedication and support, the house and its legacy was able to grow into something even more meaningful and permanent.

I purchased Frank Lloyd Wright's Bach House because I saw the opportunity for that same evolution.

I believe in giving back to the community, strengthening our neighborhoods, encouraging local economic and social growth, and supporting quality design that will last from generation to generation. Architectural preservation and ensured visitor access encourage integration of the past with not only the present but also the future. By restoring and opening the Bach House, not only have we helped develop and enhance the identity of the Rogers Park community but we have also conserved and spread incredible tradition.

And this is not wishful, inflated thinking. Online reviews and discussions with guests clearly convey that sentiment. We value their support and are so glad to be a part of the community.

When Bob Hartnett approached me with the idea to write a book on the restoration and history of the Bach House, I was immediately on board. I knew that this project could extend the reach and life of the Bach House even further. Not only would those visiting the house have a deep guide to reference, now the experience could extend to anyone, anywhere and at any time, who picked up the book.

I am grateful for the work that Bob Hartnett and the Master Wings and Hilton publishing teams have done to articulate the Bach House legacy even further.

My favorite room at the Bach House is the living room. The rich brown satin of the woodwork and its integrated furniture make it comfortable and cozy. It is great for entertaining or relaxing. I have often sat there and read, enjoying the view and atmosphere of the room.

I hope that with the following pages you will be able to share the experience: learn, be inspired, sit in that living room with me—that with this book and with the Bach House we will encourage instances of preservation, appreciation, and attention in everyone's life.

Jennifer N. Pritzker
Col (IL), IL ARNG (Retired)
President and CEO, TAWANI Enterprises
April 2019

Author's Note

Several years ago I heard a friend of mine say, "I wish I could find another book about Frank Lloyd Wright," and I thought to myself, *maybe I could write that book*. For some reason that thought has stayed with me, especially after another person I know wrote some entertaining books about the Frank Lloyd Wright buildings in Wisconsin.

I began volunteering for the Frank Lloyd Wright Trust in 2002. I started out giving tours at the Home & Studio in Oak Park, Illinois, and then I started to do tours at Unity Temple, also located in Oak Park. I find both of these buildings magical. I had heard about the Bach House, and when I retired from my career in public works, I began giving tours there as well.

The Bach House is an interesting building because on one hand it was just supposed to be a family home. On the other hand, it is full of fascinating architectural elements that were created by one of the country's most famous architects, who at the time was working on several projects across the country and even in Japan.

So here I found this noteworthy house with a curious story that no one else had really written about. My ideas from years ago started to percolate. Why couldn't I write a book about this house? I wanted to write a book that would be entertaining, and fun to read, something that anyone who toured the Bach House or who had stayed overnight might like to take home as a remembrance of their time there. I also thought that the book could be read by someone who has an interest in Wright and his architecture and wanted to add another book to their collection.

This book is presented in three parts, beginning with the story of the original owners and ending with how the building has been restored.

When I was interviewing a member of the team of architects that worked on the house's restoration, she asked me how many chapters my book was to be, and I said I had written ten chapters so far. She chuckled a little bit and said she didn't think anyone could write ten chapters about the Bach House. My publisher didn't think so either, so the book you find today has twelve chapters. Each chapter is a building block for the next, and, not unlike a house that is built on a strong foundation, the beginning of the book introduces us to the Bach family and Frank Lloyd Wright. As the story grows it is built brick by brick, just like the Bach House was. Upon the foundation the first floor is constructed and in the book we learn about how the Bachs came to Rogers Park, and how they decided to hire Frank Lloyd Wright as their architect. On the second floor we find the beautiful art glass windows Wright created for the Bach House, and as the book continues we come to learn about the delightful elements of Japanese architecture that can be found in the home. Our story tells how the house achieved landmark status and became listed on the National Register of Historic Places. We also discover how Wright blends the interior of the home with its outdoor spaces and gardens. Finally we find as the roof is put in place to protect the home and all its contents, the book ends with the story of the restoration and how the home has been secured for the future.

I have been so fortunate to have received so much help in writing this book; I have literally talked with people from across the continent. There was a college professor in Oregon; two historical society managers, one in Wisconsin and one in Maine; a librarian in Utah; an antiques store manager in Georgia; and a manager of an architectural history museum in Montreal, Canada.

I received encouragement and assistance from the family of Emil Bach's grandson, Owen Bach. I have received the support of TAWANI Enterprises, the owner of the Bach House; the firm of Harboe Architects of Chicago; and members of the Frank Lloyd Wright Trust located in Oak Park. The staff of the Frank Lloyd Wright Foundation in Arizona, and the staff at Columbia University in New York, which holds Wright's archives, were extremely helpful.

I have also been very lucky to be part of a fantastic production team composed of a project manager from TAWANI Enterprises and an editor and a marketing manager from Hilton Publishing, who have guided me through the process of actually publishing this book.

I would like to think that this book will be enjoyed by anyone who comes to experience the Bach House, and I hope those who have yet to visit will read this story and find that spark that will send them on a journey of discovery to come and see and feel and be in this wonderful home.

AUTHOR'S NOTE

As the author of this book, I was fortunate to have some very close friends, stay at the Bach House to celebrate their wedding anniversary. In order to give them some insights into the home, I gave them an early draft of the manuscript. They used the piece as a script to experience the building. Some of the comments they made to me help me realize that the ideas in the book, were coming together. They described their time in a short note to me:

> *My wife and I had a fantastic time touring the Emil Bach House with your manuscript as our guide. In every part of our walk, you drew our attention to things we would not have noticed.*
>
> *Inside the home the rooms really do appear to be larger than they actually are. When we read that "Wright used a trick to fool our minds to create this impression," we not only understood the effect; we felt almost as if we had been let in on a family secret.*
>
> *I had heard that Wright's style incorporated elements of Japanese architecture, but I never knew what those elements were. The descriptions of these features heightened our experience. Our time at the Bach House was an enchanting experience.*

I hope as you read this book you will learn a little bit about Chicago's history and the history of how American families have worked, and lived, and loved their homes. I have tried to provide the reader with an understanding of what Frank Lloyd Wright created for the Bachs and have presented just a glimpse into how Wright combined materials, light and shadows, Japanese art, and his own ingenuity to produce a style of architecture, born in Chicago, which is unique, beautiful, and truly American.

Maybe you too will use this book as your guide to experience the Bach House. If you do, I hope you are enchanted with what you find.

Now let me introduce you to Emil and Anna Bach and their architect Frank Lloyd Wright!

Bob Hartnett
February 2019

A Special Home Celebrates 100 Years

On the afternoon of June 6, 2015, a birthday party took place on the grounds of the Emil Bach House at 7415 North Sheridan Road in Rogers Park, a home designed by Frank Lloyd Wright and constructed in 1915 for Emil Bach and his wife, Anna. The nearly one hundred guests ate birthday cake, enjoyed other refreshments in the tea house, listened to live Baroque music, and were treated to tours of the home.

The Bach House, unlike many other Wright properties, sits on a small city lot amid a busy urban setting. The shape of the structure gives it dynamic qualities with the house being one of a short series of cubic, geometric, slab-roofed homes designed in the early twentieth century. The Bach House was designated a Chicago landmark on September 28, 1977, and was entered into the National Register of Historic Places on January 23, 1979.

> "...an opportunity for more than just architectural preservation to proactively address issues of urban changes and redevelopment."

The Bach family has not lived in the house since 1934, but some of the family's descendants attended the party. Also present was Col. Jennifer Pritzker, whose company, TAWANI Enterprises, had completed the house's restoration to its original design and appearance. Among the day's events were the unveiling of a gold and silver commemorative Emil Bach House coin and proclamations presented to the Frank Lloyd Wright Trust and TAWANI Enterprises by the State of Illinois.

The Emil Bach House is a Stone Heritage Property and a TAWANI Enterprises Project. TAWANI Enterprises, Inc. brings an entrepreneurial outlook to various private investments aimed at connecting people to the history they may not recognize exists in their own neighborhoods. The company's work creates opportunities for growth and knowledge and aims to help forge strong, healthy communities.

In an interview with the author, Pritzker explained that she saw the Emil Bach House as "a significant link to the past" that as an investment represented "an opportunity for more than just architectural preservation to proactively address issues of urban changes and redevelopment."

The house, Pritzker concludes, "is pretty magical."

Due to the stewardship of Pritzker and TAWANI Enterprises, the Bach House is available today for people to experience the joys of living in a Frank Lloyd Wright-designed home, even if it's only for a few days at a time. Family and friends can now commemorate their milestone events during daylong celebrations or evening social affairs at one of the most unique and special event spaces in Chicago. The Bach House offers admirers of the architecture of Frank Lloyd Wright from the casual to the scholarly an in-depth museum experience. Tours of the home provide visitors with a rare look into one of the few remaining Prairie-style Wright-designed homes in Chicago. Here visitors can experience the ambiance of a building created by Wright during that transitional period of his career between his Oak Park years and the development of his California textile block homes that preluded the Usonian styles of his later career.

Frank Lloyd Wright's $10,000 Home: History, Design, and Restoration of the Bach House will give the reader an in-depth look at how the home came to be, how it has been lived in, and how it has been reborn. You will also learn some of the secrets of Frank Lloyd Wright's design genius and get a glimpse of his process for creating spaces without walls to form a harmonious living experience between human inhabitants and the nature that surrounds them.

Opposite page: Quotation is from *Frank Lloyd Wright: The Complete 1925 "Wendingen" Series* by Frank Lloyd Wright (New York: Dover Publications, 1992)

PART ONE

THE BACH HOUSE'S FOUNDATIONS IN CHICAGO

"A building should appear to grow easily from its site and be shaped to harmonize with its surroundings if Nature is manifest there."

—Frank Lloyd Wright, 1925

CHAPTER ONE
Early Chicago and the Arrival of Wilhelm Johann Bach and Frank Lloyd Wright

THE SOUTHWESTERN SHORES OF LAKE Michigan have been inhabited since at least the early 1600s, first by Native Americans, then by European fur traders, and now by more than 9.5 million Chicagoans. While the exact origin of the name "Chicago" is not known, the most accepted explanation is that it's derived from the Miami Native American tribe's word *shikaakwa*, which means "smelly onion," likely referring to the wild leeks that grew around a stream close to the city we know today.[1]

To aid in the settlement of Chicago, the United States Army in 1803 sent Captain John Whistler, along with a garrison of men, to build a fort that he named Fort Dearborn. The city's name was officially recorded as "Chicago" in 1830 and was just under half a mile in size. The small frontier town with just over 100 residents and 1.15 miles of land was incorporated as a town in 1833. Within a few short years Chicago was officially incorporated into a city in 1837 when the population exceeded 4,000 and the city had grown to 10 square miles. Chicago eventually grew to become a major transportation hub as eastern US railroads expanded westward, and the population exploded to 300,000 by 1870.

Fires and Building Codes

Mrs. O'Leary and her poor cow have been blamed for starting what became known as "The Great Chicago Fire." While the true cause was never determined, legend holds that the cow overturned a lantern in Mrs. O'Leary's barn on Sunday, October 8, 1871, setting off a fire that burned through the city until Tuesday, October 10, torching more than three square miles and destroying more than 17,000 buildings. The fire claimed the lives of 300 people, and an estimated 100,000 residents lost their homes.

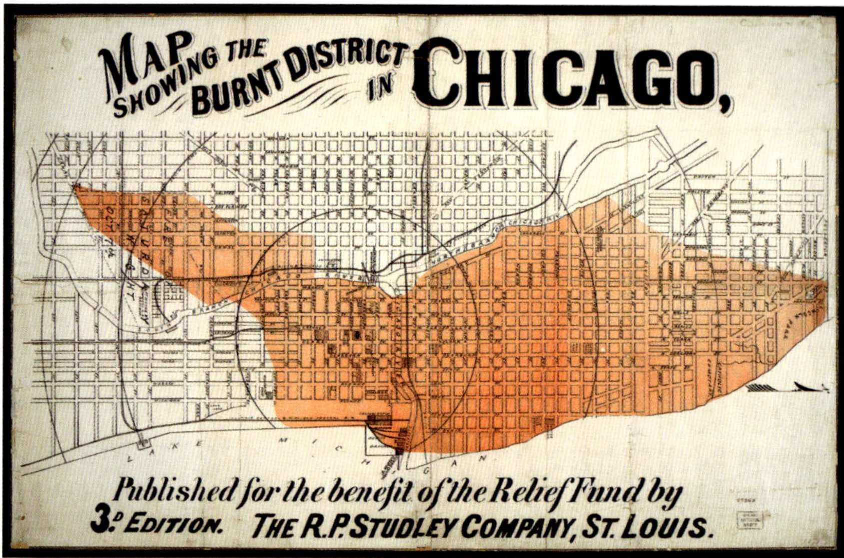

Chicago History Museum, 2011

Map of damage from 1871 Chicago fire

After the fire, the city established building codes that restricted the construction of any wooden buildings in the commercial districts downtown, and the rebuilt business district consisted of brick buildings. But it wasn't until after a second fire in 1874 that even more stringent building codes were established in Chicago. This fire was not nearly as devastating as the Great Fire, lasting only seven hours and burning itself out when it reached the new brick construction. However, in the fire's aftermath, insurance companies canceled policies and warned the city's government that they would not provide coverage until the city's fire protection and prevention services were upgraded. The city responded by banning all wooden building construction throughout the city, increasing the size of the underground water mains, and professionalizing the Chicago Fire Department.

These fires and the need for more brick buildings and architects to design them produced two seemingly unrelated moments in the city's history. First, in 1881, Wilhelm Johann Bach, a German potter and brick maker, began what would become a thriving brick business in Chicago. And second, in 1887, Frank Lloyd Wright left the University of Wisconsin before earning a degree and moved to Chicago to begin his career as an architect.

CHAPTER TWO
The Bach Family Builds a Brick Manufacturing Company

By the early 1890s, there were more than sixty brickyards in and around Chicago that produced close to 600 million bricks a year. Wilhelm Johann Bach (1832–1911) had learned the trade of brick manufacturing in the town of Plochingen, Germany. In 1860 he married Maria Katharina Hägele, and shortly thereafter their family blossomed to a brood of nine children, including six boys and three girls: Wilhelm, Friedrich, Julius, Wilhelmine, Karl Heinrich, Karl Otto (who went by his middle name most of his life), Sophie, Emil, and Marie. In 1881 the Bach family immigrated to Chicago, settling in the Lakeview neighborhood.

Wilhelm soon established the Wm. Bach Manufacturer of Brick and Tile company. He changed his name to the more American-sounding William in 1895, and the company became William Bach and Sons, Inc. The company name changed once again in 1905 to Bach Brick Company after William retired. As the business grew, new sources for clay deposits needed to be found, and the family moved their brick manufacturing operation from one Chicago neighborhood to another before finally settling on the 53-acre site

Courtesy of Owen Bach family

Emil Bach's business card

Courtesy of Owen Bach family

A Bach brick with its signature diamond

at 2647 Montrose Avenue. This location, which is now the site of Horner Park, is bordered by the Chicago River to the east, California Avenue to the west, and Irving Park Road to the south.

The company excavated the clays that were left in the Chicago area after the last Ice Age, and the bricks they made were called Chicago common bricks. These bricks had an orange or pink color and were used to pave roads and construct buildings during the late 1800s and early 1900s. Each brick included the Bach family name and a rhombus-like diamond shape.

The Bach Brothers

Eventually, all six of William Bach's sons worked at the brick manufacturing company. By 1903, the company employed fifty people. Between 1903 and 1934, Julius Bach was issued several patents for inventing apparatuses that improved the brick manufacturing process. Henry Bach, the president of the company in 1923, declared, "The present outlook for the common brick business is favorable."

The Move to Rogers Park

With its rural farm-like charm and Lake Michigan as its eastern boundary, Rogers Park became one of the North Shore's most desired neighborhoods for the self-made businessmen of Chicago. These prosperous families had the financial means to move away from the city center, where the smells from

©Science, Industry & Business Library / The New York Public Library / American Clay Magazine

The Bach brothers in *American Clay Magazine*, July 1913

factories and the smoke from coal-fired trains saturated the air. Chicago's ever-expanding systems of "L" trains and streetcars enabled people to breeze into work and also to continue to shop on State Street.

> **"There also has been a tendency among the wealthier class to seek permanent homes away from the noise and bustle of the city. This fact is evidenced in the settlement of the fashionable and attractive North Shore suburbs, such as Lake Forest, Highland Park, Glencoe, Winnetka, Hubbard Woods, Kenilworth, and Lake Bluff, and in Rogers Park and Edgewater, farther south."**
>
> **—*Chicago Tribune*, 1911**

Because the family business was thriving, Otto Bach began looking for a new home, which he found in Chicago's Rogers Park neighborhood. Otto Bach and his wife Louise became part of the growing migration to the northern neighborhoods, and in 1912 they purchased a Frank Lloyd Wright-designed Prairie-style home formerly owned by Oscar and Katherine Steffens. Mr. Steffens had also been involved in the Chicago brick industry.

CHAPTER THREE
Frank Lloyd Wright Helps Create a New American Style of Architecture

FRANK LLOYD WRIGHT ARRIVED IN Chicago in 1887 and took employment as a draftsman in the office of architect Joseph Lyman Silsbee. Wright worked for Silsbee for about a year, and by 1888 he was working for the firm of Adler and Sullivan. Wright had found partner Louis Sullivan's ideas of a uniquely American-style of architecture very captivating, and he soon found himself Sullivan's protégé.

Louis Sullivan

Frank Lloyd Wright

In 1893, however, Wright was forced to leave Adler and Sullivan after he was caught designing homes outside the limitations of his exclusive contract with the firm. Wright had designed at least nine different homes in 1891 and 1893. These "bootleg" houses, as they have come to be known, can be found in the villages of Oak Park and La Grange, Illinois, and in the Kenwood neighborhood of Chicago. Rather than securing contracts between the firm and the homeowners, as he was required to do, he contracted with these clients on his own, likely designing these homes in his second-floor studio at

Wright's Oak Park home and studio, Oak Park, Illinois

his Oak Park home, a room he later turned into bedrooms for his children. After leaving the firm, Wright established his own practice with offices in the Schiller Building in downtown Chicago, where he worked until 1889, when he moved to his newly designed studio adjoining his Oak Park home.

Prairie School Architecture

Wright believed that if a man lived in a beautiful home, his life would be improved, and his clients believed this as well. His desire to create a new style of architecture that promoted this idea was the genesis of the Prairie School. The Prairie School style of architecture was developed in the late 1800s and flourished until the early 1900s. The rise of this design philosophy was promoted by a group of Chicago-based architects, including Wright, and led by Louis Sullivan.[2]

The Prairie School was advanced by architects who had similar ideas as disciples of the Arts and Crafts movement. Both Arts and Crafts designers and Prairie School architects preferred that individual craftsmen create handmade objects such as furniture, ceramic vases, or copper cookware rather than homeowners purchasing such items that were mass-produced. Although Wright believed in most of the principles associated with the Prairie School, such as open floor plans and designs based on nature, he did not have a disdain for machine-made items. In his speech "The Art and Craft of the Machine" at a 1901 meeting of the Chicago Arts and Crafts Society, he proposed that the machine could free man from laborious tasks and provide him with more time to be with his family in his beautiful Wright-designed home.

For Wright, any object in a home—a chair, a vase, or even a window—needed to be designed as part of the whole building. Each item, in its own way, contributed to the experience of living in a Prairie-style home.

He wanted to break away from Victorian-style homes that were overly ornamental and had multicolored exteriors with siding that was scalloped or shingled. Victorian homes featured roofs with steep gables and towers or turrets protruding from the building, as well as interior rooms that were small and closed off by single doorways. Wright's inspiration came from the American prairies of his youth, and his buildings were designed to emulate the horizontal line of the prairie. He used both hip roofs with long, low, sheltering eaves, and flat roof designs that were cantilevered beyond the walls to provide the same sheltering effect. His art glass windows were created with three simple tools: the T-square, the triangle, and his beloved colored pencils. The materials he chose for his buildings were unadorned and natural. Wood trim was unstained and never painted; bricks and stone added earth-tone colors; stucco exteriors had minimal color; interior walls could be painted, or even wallpapered, but were never gaudy. Interior spaces flowed together; areas were defined by partitions or furniture groupings and not necessarily by walls.

Prairie School architects wanted to cultivate an authentic style of architecture for the United States; they shunned architectural features found in European building designs, such as elaborate trim, sash windows, wrap-around porches, and bright colors. Based on the teachings of Louis Sullivan, Prairie School architects would try to use natural elements to adorn buildings.

Natural materials such as wood and stone were used and admired for their intrinsic characteristics. The straight-grained and coarse texture of oak became a popular choice of Prairie School designers, and these wooden surfaces were left unpainted so that their natural beauty could be seen. A distinguishing feature in the design of a Prairie-style home was a sloping roof with wide sheltering eaves cantilevered beyond the vertical wall supports.

Very often a hip roof was employed, leading all four sides of the roof to slope down from a central ridge line to the walls.

However, Wright would not let his imagination be limited to one style of roof. If you were to take a stroll south from Wright's Oak Park home and studio, from the corner of Chicago and Forest avenues, you'd first encounter his design for the Arthur B. Heurtley House (1902), with its hip roof, and as you continued south on Forest and just after you crossed Elizabeth Court you'd find the Peter A. Beachy House (1906) with a roof designed with multiple gables. Turning back north, if you were to take a right turn on Elizabeth Court, as you walked down the gently curving street you would find the Laura Gale House (1904) complete with its flat roof and cantilevered balconies.

Wright's use of different materials for the exterior façade of his homes was also common. He used stucco, brick, and wood in many different combinations. The common feature regardless of the façade's makeup was that the colors would be natural, and the horizontal lines of Midwestern Prairie-style homes would be accentuated by wood trim or masonry features. It was also typical for Wright to include an open porch or balcony to provide an easy transition between the interior of the home and nature.

Prairie-style homes would have uniquely designed art glass windows whose patterns depicted stylized natural elements and were often arranged in horizontal bands. These art glass designs acted as screens to shield the homeowners from the gaze of pedestrians rather than using window shades. The hearth and inglenook (a nook by a fireplace including a bench or a settle) would be a central feature of the first-floor suite of rooms, which would encircle the chimney and flow into each other seamlessly. Partitions, half-height walls, or furniture would define separate spaces. Walls would evaporate from sight with the use of trim boards, which would surround the room and travel down the adjoining corners to soften the view. The Prairie School architect endeavored to break up boxy Victorian interiors. Frank Lloyd Wright believed that the spaces where people lived were more important than the exterior walls of a building, once stating, "The space within becomes the reality of the building."[3]

Wright's experiments in trying to define a truly American style of architecture finally came to fruition with the B. Harley Bradley House (1900), located in Kankakee, Illinois. This home, set along the banks of the Kankakee River with its broad overhanging roof, strong horizontal lines, art glass windows, and open floor plan, has come to be known as the first building that expresses Wright's Prairie School vision.

Courtesy of Wright in Kankakee

B. Harley Bradley House, Kankakee, Illinois

Determining Wright's "last" Prairie-style home is a little more difficult. In *Frank Lloyd Wright Prairie Homes* by Allan Weintraub and Allen Hess, the last home listed is the American System-Built Home constructed for Charles Heisen, located in Villa Park, Illinois, built in 1920. However, Wright himself called Herbert F. Johnson's 1937 home, Wingspread, in Racine, Wisconsin, "...the last of the Prairie houses."[4]

Courtesy of Citywide Services Real Estate Appraisers

Charles Heisen House, Villa Park, Illinois

Courtesy of the Johnson Foundation at Wingspread

Wingspread, Racine, Wisconsin

Wright Builds in Rogers Park

The land adjacent to the Birchwood Country Club in Rogers Park became highly desirable to builders, and development in the area between Sheridan Road and Lake Michigan began in the early 1900s. It was in this neighborhood that two of Frank Lloyd Wright's clients chose to build their Prairie-style homes: the L. K. Horner House in 1908 and the Oscar Steffens House in 1909.

Courtesy of Douglas M. Steiner

L. K. Horner House, Chicago, Illinois (demolished 1952)

The Horner House was a smaller version of Wright's Prairie-style homes, but he incorporated many Prairie School features in this home, including broad overhangs, balconies, terraces, and built-in planters on the exterior. The house included built-in cabinets and furniture in the interior along with rich oak trim, which created distinctive horizontal lines. Wright designed the home's art glass windows and light fixtures, and of course there was a large, centrally located fireplace on the first floor. The home's façade was stucco, and the balconies were trimmed in wood.

The Horner home was approximately three-and-one-half blocks south of the eventual location of the Emil Bach home, so is quite plausible that the Bachs knew of this house when they were planning their own home.

Courtesy of Douglas M. Steiner

Oscar Steffens House, Chicago, Illinois (demolished 1963)

The Steffens House was larger than the Horner House and included an entrance that was slightly obscured, which compelled visitors to travel Wright's "path of discovery" to enter the home. The house was constructed from a cream-colored stucco, had dark horizontal wood trim on the exterior, and sat on a pronounced water table, which assisted in directing water away from the foundation. [5]

After Otto and Louise Bach moved into the Steffens House in Rogers Park, Otto's brother Emil visited frequently, and he developed a deep appreciation for this Prairie-style house. Emil's admiration for this home led him to seek out Frank Lloyd Wright in 1915 to design a home for his own family.

A New Phase for Wright

Hiring Frank Lloyd Wright as their architect was probably as satisfying for the Bachs as it was for Wright, because by 1915 his architectural practice had been severely diminished. In 1909, Wright left Oak Park and traveled to Berlin, Germany, to work on a book titled *Ausgeführte Bauten und Entwürfe*

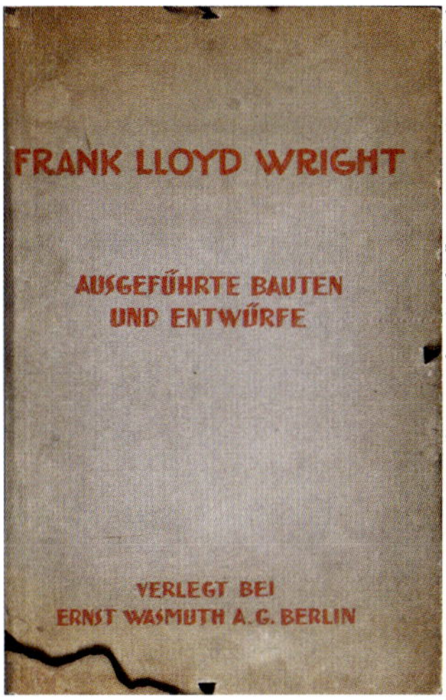

Courtesy of Marriott Library Special Collections Division / University of Utah

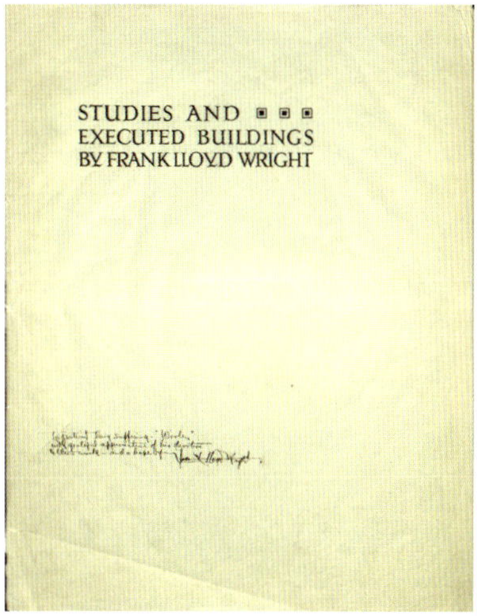

Courtesy of Neal Auction Company

The Wasmuth Portfolio

von Frank Lloyd Wright (Executed Buildings and Designs by Frank Lloyd Wright). The book has come to be known as The Wasmuth Portfolio after its German publisher, Ernst Wasmuth. This work was published in 1910, printed as a two-volume set that included 100 lithographs of the intact buildings Frank Lloyd Wright created from 1893 to 1909. It was the first time Wright's work had been published anywhere in the world.

Between 1909 and 1910, Wright traveled extensively throughout Europe and spent many months in both Florence and Fiesole, Italy, where he maintained homes with Mamah Borthwick Cheney, his beloved mistress.

Mamah Borthwick Cheney

Frank Lloyd Wright had designed a home in Oak Park for Edwin and Marta (Mamah) Cheney in 1903, a mere eight blocks from Wright's own home and studio. Frank and Mamah's affair may have begun during the time the home was being designed and constructed, if not shortly thereafter. They were less than secretive about their affair, according to Brendan Gill in his book *Many Masks: A Life of Frank Lloyd Wright:* "Wright and Mrs. Cheney, both champions of 'advanced ideas,' saw fit to discuss their affair at length with their respective spouses, Catherine Wright and Edwin Cheney."

Mamah Borthwick Cheney

In October of 1909 Mamah left home with her children to visit a friend in Boulder, Colorado. Shortly thereafter, she cabled her husband to come and pick up the children as her friend had passed away.[6] When Edwin arrived in Boulder, he found his wife had spirited herself away to New York.

Meanwhile, Wright had been busy finalizing plans to travel to Germany to work on his new venture. He turned his office over to a young German architect named Hermann von Holst, who, along with some other remaining employees and a few former architects of the firm, closed out the active commissions.[7] Wright borrowed money, took advances on pending commissions, and sold several of his precious Japanese art prints to fund his and Mamah's voyage and subsequent travels to Europe.

When Mamah arrived in New York, she joined Wright, and together they began their journey posing as husband and wife. Upon arriving in Germany they registered at the Hotel Adlon as Mr. and Mrs. Wright.[8]

Wright's relationship with Mamah led to scandal, which significantly damaged his architectural practice.

No one is sure exactly how the *Chicago Tribune's* Berlin office staff found out the two lovers had arrived in Berlin, but when the news broke it was sensational.

The headline from the *Tribune's* Sunday edition on November 7, 1909, reporting on Wright's scandalous affair, read:

LEAVE FAMILIES; ELOPE TO EUROPE
Architect Frank Lloyd Wright and Mrs. Edwin Cheney
of Oak Park Startle Friends.
ABANDONED WIFE LOYAL.

This article, along with others printed at the time, vilified the couple. In Frank Lloyd Wright's autobiography he tells us how Oak Park was also referred to as "Saint's Rest" because there were so many churches there. However, after the news of his "elopement" broke, Pastor Frederick H. Hopkins of the Pilgrim Congregational Church in Oak Park performed a sermon that mixed any number of barnyard images finally linking Frank and Mamah. [9]

Having left his office in 1909, Wright found it difficult to rebuild his practice upon his return the following year. The scandal of his affair when it was discovered in Germany was damaging enough, but his staunch refusal to go back to his wife and family upon his return just reignited the gossip and rumors.

In Gill's biography of Wright he stated, "If Wright's running off to Europe with Mrs. Cheney was a well publicized scandal and seemed to put an end to a professional career of exceptional brilliance, his return was also in a sense a scandal, because he made it clear that he was preparing for a new stage in his life with his now celebrated mistress."

Gill suggested that many of Wright's clients pre-1910 had been people who wanted a different style of home, something that wasn't conventional. Wright won over women clients first and then their husbands, who were willing to take a risk on building a Prairie School house in a neighborhood with Victorian or Colonial homes on the same block. Now these same clients were shying away from Wright. American morals still dictated who a family man and his wife should be associating with, and Wright's newfound fame and dubious standing in the community made him the last person they would want walking up to their front door.

Having no current projects to return to and not having the means to support himself or his family financially, Wright turned to his old friend from Buffalo, New York—Darwin Martin.

Wright had worked with Martin on several projects in Buffalo, including the Barton House (for Darwin's sister) and the Darwin Martin House, both in 1903; one of Wright's early masterpieces, the Larkin Soap Company

Administration Building (1904); and finally, a home for the Martin family's gardener (1908).

Rather than working for Darwin Martin, Wright cajoled and prodded him into being his financial benefactor. Between 1910 and 1911, Wright secured a loan from Martin to pay for an installment on the publication of his German portfolio. He then told Martin his mother had bought a farm in Wisconsin and she was short on cash because she hadn't sold her Oak Park home, which Martin then assumed the mortgage for, and finally Wright received another $25,000 loan from Martin for living expenses. [10]

Taliesin

Amongst the borrowing and persuading, Wright was making plans to build a home in Spring Green, Wisconsin, not far from his birthplace, Richland Center. Initially he said that the Spring Green home, eventually named Taliesin, was to be for his mother, but in a letter to Darwin Martin in January of 1912, Wright listed his address as Taliesin, making it clear that he had retained the home as his own residence.

Wisconsin Historical Society

Taliesin, Spring Green, Wisconsin

It was from here that Wright began to rebuild his career. After his return from Europe, he closed his Oak Park studio and opened a new set of offices in the prestigious Orchestra Hall building, located across the street from the Art Institute on Chicago's trendy Michigan Avenue. Wright's Oak Park office and studio had opened in 1889, and between that year and its 1911 closure he completed 105 commissions. However, after his return from Europe and amid his scandalous affair he completed only thirty-three commissions between 1911 and 1915. One of Wright's largest projects was the Midway Gardens entertainment complex in Chicago, built in 1914, but besides that facility he completed only two other projects that year.

The year 1914 was a tragic one for Frank Lloyd Wright: While he was in Chicago overseeing the construction of Midway Gardens, Mamah, her two children, and four of Wright's employees were murdered at Taliesin by servant Julian Carlton, who then set Wright's beloved Wisconsin home ablaze, reducing large portions of the building to ashes. Wright was devastated, but he found solace in his work.

After this tragedy, Wright completed twenty-six buildings in 1915, including fourteen American System-Built Homes, which were designed by Wright for a developer named Arthur L. Richards. Another ten structures were constructed in Sherman Booth's Ravine Bluffs development in Glencoe, Illinois. This development included six Wright-designed homes, three identical concrete sculptures, and one bridge.

Five of the houses in the Ravine Bluffs development shared the basic floor plan of Wright's famous design for "A Fireproof House for $5,000," an article by Wright published in *Ladies' Home Journal* in April of 1907. Another home built in Glencoe but not part of the Ravine Bluffs development was the Edmund F. Brigham House, designed by Wright between 1908 and 1909 but not constructed until 1915.

Wright also began two commercial projects in 1915. The first was the A. D. German Warehouse, located in Richland Center, Wisconsin. The early designs for this building date from 1915, but the building was not finished until 1921. The second project Wright worked on in 1915 was his first international commission—the Imperial Hotel in Tokyo, Japan, completed in 1923.

© Peter Van Vechten

© Peter Van Vechten

© Peter Van Vechten

Thus, the only custom-built home that Frank Lloyd Wright completely designed and had constructed in 1915 was the home for Emil and Anna Bach. It shared a distinct characteristic with the American System-Built Homes project: Wright designed it for a family of moderate income.

The number of commissions for Prairie School architects began to wane after 1914. Some of the factors that contributed to its demise were the onset of World War I and the fact that three of the leading Prairie School architects left the United States—Wright for Japan, and Walter Burley Griffin and Marion Mahony for Australia. The departure of the magazine *House Beautiful* from Chicago to the eastern United States and the folding of the magazine *Craftsman* in 1916 also contributed to the decline in popularity of the Prairie School.[11]

Opposite page (from top): A house, bridge, and sculpture from the Ravine Bluffs development in Glencoe, Illinois

Opposite page: Quotation is from *An Autobiography* by Frank Lloyd Wright (London, New York: Longmans, Green & Co., 1932)

PART TWO

THE BACH HOUSE'S HISTORY, EVOLUTION, AND CULTURAL SIGNIFICANCE

"If Japanese prints were to be deducted from my education, I don't know what direction the whole would have taken."

—Frank Lloyd Wright, 1932

CHAPTER FOUR
Emil and Anna Bach Build a Home in Rogers Park

ON FEBRUARY 17, 1904, TWENTY-EIGHT-YEAR-OLD Emil Bach married Anna M. Diers, who was twenty-three and hailed from Santa Ana, California.

By 1910 Emil and Anna were living on Montrose Avenue in Chicago, on the site of the Bach family's brickyard. Emil had already developed the desire to build his own home elsewhere, inspired by the Wright-designed home of his brother Otto in Rogers Park.[12] Emil and Anna discovered a vacant lot for sale on Sheridan Road in that neighborhood. The site was approximately two blocks west of Lake Michigan. On December 5, 1914, they purchased this site for their future home.

Wedding photo of Emil and Anna Bach

The Design

According to the original correspondence between the Bachs and Frank Lloyd Wright, the Bachs' home was designed in Wright's Orchestra Hall offices. The origins of the Bach House scheme can be discovered by researching other building designs Wright used. Applying the lessons he learned as a child while working with the Froebel blocks his mother had given him,

Wright ingeniously melded three unique design concepts into one compact building. These three concepts came from Wright's *Ladies' Home Journal* article "A Fireproof House for $5,000," an architectural study Wright called "Study for a Small Suburban House," and, surprisingly, from the belvedere designs for Midway Gardens.

The *ukiyo-e* style drawing Wright included in his article for the fireproof house show a home fashioned as a cube set upon a water table, with a projected planter below a set of banded art glass windows and a flat, cantilevered roof. There also seems to be a trellis feature just below the second-floor windows. Each of these characteristics are replicated in the Bach House.

AntiqueHomeStyle.com

Wright's Fireproof House

The "Fireproof House" would have been a compact, durable home. The home's design included the essential features that a family with a moderate income would find necessary, yet the building would also have decorative accents such as beautiful art glass windows, trellises, and gardens. Wright believed that each person's life could be enhanced by living in a home that was as beautiful as it was functional. Even though an exact replica of the "Fireproof House" was never built, Wright designed several homes using a similar geometric cubic shape, a flat roof, and overhanging eaves. Examples of some of these homes include the Laura Gale House (1909) in Oak Park, Illinois, the Oscar B. Balch House (1911), also in Oak Park, the Coonley Playhouse in Riverside, Illinois (1912), and the Frederick C. Bogk House (1916), in Milwaukee, Wisconsin.

The "Study"

During his seven-decade career, Wright designed 532 buildings that were in fact built, but he also created hundreds of sketches and designs for other buildings that were never constructed. Some of these designs were for commissions that never got off the ground for a variety of reasons, but other projects were architectural studies. Wright used these working drawings to flesh out his ideas or to investigate certain concepts. One such study that Wright created in 1911 or 1912 was "Study for a Small Suburban House," now cataloged in the Frank Lloyd Wright Archives. The drawing is for a first-floor concept only, and this building was not designed for any specific location; the plan sheet can be found in the book *Frank Lloyd Wright: Complete Works, Vol. 1, 1885-1916*, by Peter Gossel and Bruce Brooks Pfeiffer.

The text included with this plan sheet, which was written by Pfeiffer, the director of the Frank Lloyd Wright Archives from 1959 to 2017, states the following: "The plan matches, with minor alterations, the house for Emil Bach in Chicago, 1915. It is a square, again on the lines of the 'Fireproof House' with an enclosed porch off the entry hall."

The building on the plan sheet has many of the attributes found in the Bach House, including a living room that is projected beyond the main building, a built-in dining table that extends into the living room, and an obscured entryway. Even the inglenook appears to have an inverted brick designed hearth. The exterior design of this home includes gardens on the front and sides of the house, with a garden wall separating the front side yard and the rear yard, and there is an enclosed porch, just like the Bach House.

The Second Floor Plan

The roof and trellis plan is based on a scheme Wright created the previous year. Author Paul Kruty states, "The exterior composition of the Emil Bach residence is a virtual recreation of one of the [Midway Gardens] belvederes."[13]

While the design of Midway Gardens is extremely ornate and detailed, the Bach House is subtler; the trellis, balconies, and overhanging roof lines are evident in both structures.

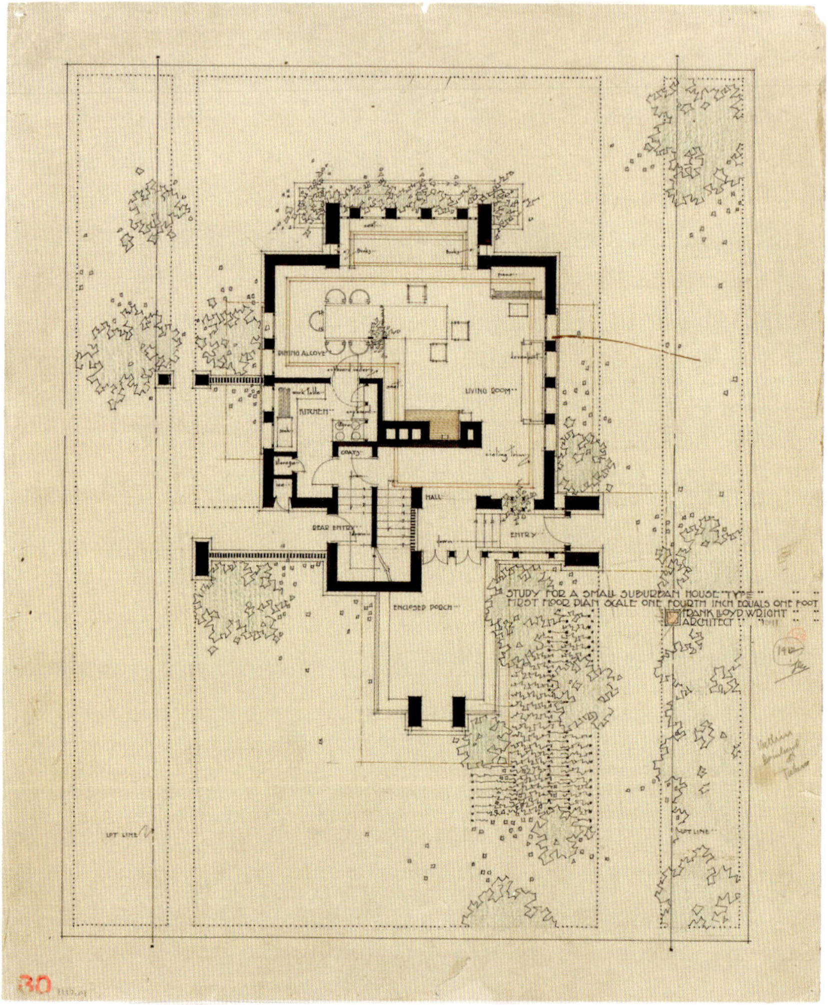

Frank Lloyd Wright Foundation Archives / Museum of Modern Art / Avery Architectural and Fine Arts Library, Columbia University

Floor plan of 1911 study

The cross-axial plan of the house, the combination of the vertical piers on the first floor and the cantilevered balconies, and the flat roof illustrate that the Bach House was born out of the massing of Froebel blocks and tiles to create a multi-level cube-like Prairie School building that Wright created by merging several clever ideas into one.

Courtesy of Douglas M. Steiner

Midway Gardens

Courtesy of Harboe Architects

Cross-axial view of the Bach House prior to the 2010 restoration

The Presentation Drawings

At some point in early 1915, Frank Lloyd Wright created at least three presentation drawings of the Bach house. These drawings are now housed in the permanent collection of the Canadian Centre for Architecture in Montreal (CCA). The CCA acquired the drawings in 1980 from Wilbert Hasbrouck, the owner of the Prairie Avenue Bookshop in Chicago. The first drawing shows the west elevation of the home. It is a three-panel *ukiyo-e* style drawing, with the house centered in the main panel and the two side panels showing natural surroundings. The drawing evokes the sense of a lone house on the prairie, not the urban setting we find the house in today. The lower right-hand corner provides us with some information about the drawing. The words are handwritten in a distinctive style that is difficult to duplicate with today's modern fonts. The bullet points between each word are red, and Wright's red square signature block is clearly visible. Unfortunately, the drawings are not dated.

MR. • EMIL • BACH •
STUDY • FOR • DWELLING •
FRANK • LLOYD • WRIGHT •
ARCHITECT •

The next drawing includes the same type of title but adds the words

FIRST • FLOOR • PLAN

This drawing includes some interesting handwritten notes, which suggests that these drawings were reviewed by the Bachs with Wright, or if not with Frank Lloyd Wright himself, possibly his son John. In this drawing, the house is noticeably centered on the site. Two sets of wooden fences extend from the house to the north. One fence is situated at about the midpoint of the house, and the second fence is near the rear of the building. The fence that extends south is on the drawing, but there are scribbled pencil lines over this section as if to show it being eliminated. The final blueprints include the one fence that extends north at the house's midpoint, but the prints also include the porthole-style fence that extends south. The blueprints also include an option for a different style fence than the porthole fence. This design was made up of simple vertical slats. It seems that the Bachs did not care for this style as they opted for the porthole-style fence instead.

CHAPTER FOUR

Frank Lloyd Wright Foundation / Canadian Centre for Architecture

Presentation drawing by Frank Lloyd Wright, front elevation

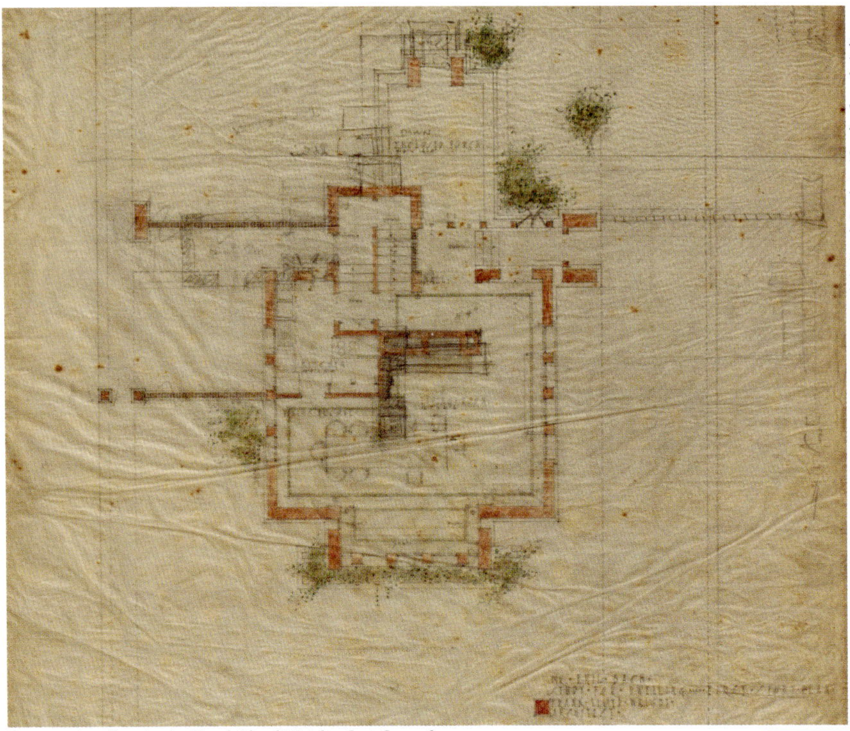

Frank Lloyd Wright Foundation / Canadian Centre for Architecture

Presentation drawing by Frank Lloyd Wright, first floor plan

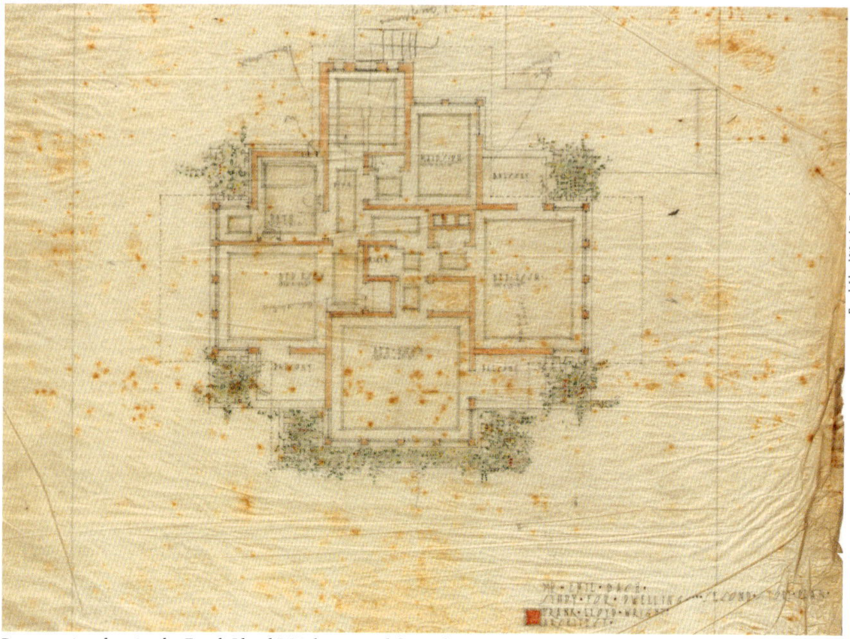

Frank Lloyd Wright Foundation / Canadian Centre for Architecture

Presentation drawing by Frank Lloyd Wright, second floor plan

There are two other interesting penciled-in attributes on this drawing. The first is at the entryway on the southeast corner of the home. The drawing clearly depicts that the way to the entrance is from the south through a pillared, protected walkway. The steps leading to the main floor are at the doorway, not inside the lower landing. The drawing shows some pencil lines that look like a double door swinging open, facing east. The blueprints show the entryway as being constructed as it is today, with the door to the east and the steps inside the landing. The area where the pillared walkway was originally shown is now a glass-enclosed atrium, which still includes the cantilevered wooden trellis that can be seen on the first drawing. The second interesting feature is a penciled-in set of exterior stairs that lead out from the interior stairway landing up to the second-floor sun porch, suggesting that this porch access may have been the Bachs' idea and not a Wright-designed feature.

Other differences between this drawing and the actual house include the inglenook, which is shown without the bookcase, and the seat at the fireplace is built-in and bordered by wall sections on the north and south sides. The brickwork at the fireplace is also different in that it extends in front of the bench seat lengthwise, not parallel with the front of the fireplace. The chairs shown on the drawing at the dining/buffet table include three cubed-back chairs and five curved-back chairs. The blueprints include details for six similar cane-back chairs, one with side armrests. There is no flower box noted on the drawing behind the built-in couch in the living room, but this feature is noted on the blueprints.

The third and final drawing is the plan for the second floor. This drawing does not show any built-in furniture in the bedrooms, but it does include a handwritten note for a mirror on the door of the guest bedroom; this detail is seen on the final blueprints. The second-floor art glass windows are not shown in any of these presentation drawings, but these windows are shown on the final plans.

On this third drawing, the shape of the second-floor bathroom is shown as a six-sided polygon, while on the blueprints for the home the bathroom is a rectangle, and the area that had made up the polygon is now used as an alcove in the child's bedroom to locate the built-in desk.

These drawings provide some interesting insight into how the home was created in partnership between the Bachs and Frank Lloyd Wright.

The Cost

It is hard to say what the Bachs might have told Wright about their proposed budget for the design and construction of their new home. We can assume that they were not

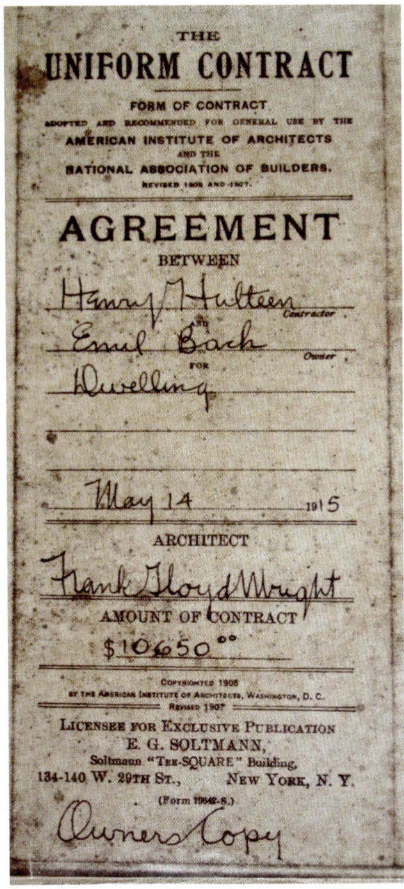
THE
UNIFORM CONTRACT
FORM OF CONTRACT
AMERICAN INSTITUTE OF ARCHITECTS
AND THE
NATIONAL ASSOCIATION OF BUILDERS.
REVISED 1905 AND 1907.
AGREEMENT
BETWEEN
Henry Hulteen Contractor
AND
Emil Bach Owner
FOR
Dwelling
May 14 1915
ARCHITECT
Frank Lloyd Wright
AMOUNT OF CONTRACT
$10650.00
COPYRIGHTED 1905
BY THE AMERICAN INSTITUTE OF ARCHITECTS, WASHINGTON, D. C.
REVISED 1907
LICENSEE FOR EXCLUSIVE PUBLICATION
E. G. SOLTMANN,
Soltmann "TEE-SQUARE" Building,
134-140 W. 29TH ST., NEW YORK, N. Y.
(Form [illegible])
Owners Copy

Courtesy of Owen Bach family

Bach House construction contract

planning to spend more than $10,000 when the cost of a home in 1915 was about $3,200.[14] However, according to the Uniform Contract Agreement dated May 14, 1915, and signed by Emil Bach and Frank Lloyd Wright, the cost to build the home as designed was $10,650.

This amount was also higher than both estimates that had been received prior to the contract being signed. In two separate letters, the prices quoted for the home's construction were $9,026 and $9,700 respectively.

The first estimate is mentioned in an undated letter from John Lloyd Wright—Frank Lloyd Wright's second-eldest son, who in 1915 was working in Wright's Orchestra Hall office. John Wright states in his letter, "The complete bid for your house omitting porch, fence wall and rear terrace cover is $9,026.00, these parts to be built on within two years for an additional $767.00."

In Wright's letter to Emil Bach dated February 16, 1915 (from Los Angeles, California), he states, "John tells me that $9,700.00 without hardware was the lowest bid received but that it was from one of the most desirable contractors on the North Shore."

In each letter, Emil Bach is strongly encouraged to build the complete home soon. John Wright urges him to act by saying, "You should take advantage of the low figure at once; as I do not feel that I can hold the contractor much longer."

In Frank Lloyd Wright's letter, he also offers options for eliminating certain elements of the home's construction to lower the cost, such as changing the brick work to stucco. He even suggests he is willing to complete an "...entirely new set of plans."

In Wright's letter to the Bachs in February of 1915, he mentions, "I think by talking to [Henry] Hulteen and making some modifications the house could probably be built, including furniture complete and architect's fees for $10,000."

Frank Lloyd Wright had the uncanny ability to charm his clients into accepting his designs regardless of their cost. The final discussions between the

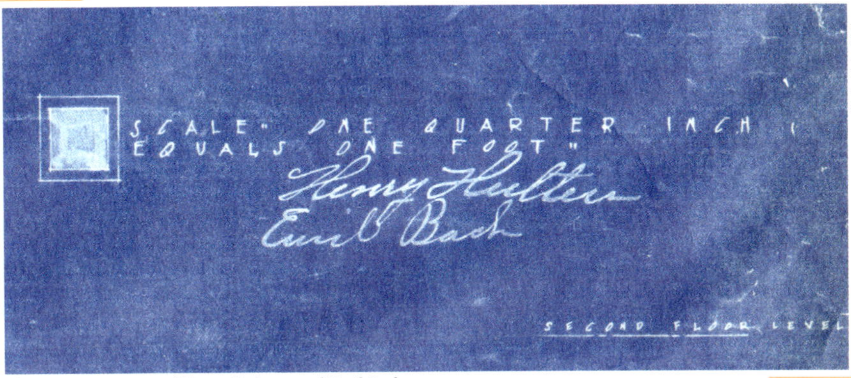

Art Institute of Chicago

Blueprint signatures of Henry Hulteen and Emil Bach, and Wright's distinctive shaded square signature block

Bachs and the Wrights (father and son), are unknown; nevertheless, Frank Lloyd Wright wooed them into spending more than even he had estimated.

The Construction

The Bach House contract was for a 2,700-square foot, two-story house, including several pieces of built-in furniture and six dining chairs. The contract was signed in May of 1915 and the construction permit, costing $2.00, was issued one month later. Henry Hulteen was a carpenter and general contractor who, along with James Wigginton, another locally based contractor, were the builders of the Bachs' home. From Wright's letter to Emil Bach we know that Wright and Hulteen had been in contact, and Hulteen had signed the original building contract for the house. Wright's unique square cubed signature design is printed on each of the blueprint pages. Henry Hulteen and Emil Bach each have signed the blueprint pages as confirmation of their approval of the design.

However, it was James Wigginton who had signed for the City of Chicago building permit, which was issued on June 12, 1915.

Surely these men would have known each other. Both Hulteen and Wigginton lived in Evanston, Illinois, their residences were four blocks apart, and they each lived about two-and-one-half miles north of the Bach House location. In addition, they had shared construction duties on the 1916 Robert A. Worstall office building[15] and another building project by Arthur Howell Knox, a Chicago-based architect, in 1921.[16]

Hulteen advertised his business as one that gave "estimates cheerfully." James Wigginton's business advertisement in the Evanston telephone directory was certainly more perfunctory, but it did provide all the necessary information to any prospective client.

Northwestern University Archives

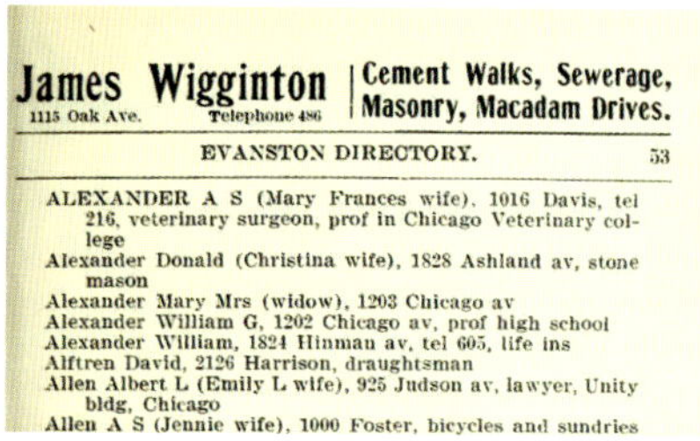

EVANSTON DIRECTORY. 53

ALEXANDER A S (Mary Frances wife), 1016 Davis, tel 216, veterinary surgeon, prof in Chicago Veterinary college
Alexander Donald (Christina wife), 1828 Ashland av, stone mason
Alexander Mary Mrs (widow), 1203 Chicago av
Alexander William G, 1202 Chicago av, prof high school
Alexander William, 1824 Hinman av, tel 605, life ins
Alftren David, 2126 Harrison, draughtsman
Allen Albert L (Emily L wife), 925 Judson av, lawyer, Unity bldg, Chicago
Allen A S (Jennie wife), 1000 Foster, bicycles and sundries

Northwestern University Archives

Advertisements for contractors Henry Hulteen and James Wigginton

According to City of Chicago Building Department reports, the inspections for the excavation work at the home site were completed on Friday, June 12, 1915, and the foundation was inspected four days later. Within a few weeks the first floor was complete, having been inspected on Friday, July 23. The roof inspection was completed on Thursday, August 19. In just under fourteen weeks, the exterior of the house was completed. The final inspection report was dated Wednesday, January 19, 1916.

Emil Bach, having enjoyed his brother's Prairie-style home, wanted a similar design for himself, and he found a design by Frank Lloyd Wright that would perfectly suit him and his small family. Maybe the cost was more than he initially wanted to spend, but ultimately he had the Prairie-style house he wanted in the fashionable suburb of Rogers Park.

CHAPTER FIVE
The Finished Bach Home

The Bachs moved into their finished house in 1916. The features of this Wright-designed structure set it apart as a work of art as well as a fully functional home. Emil and Anna Bach lived there with their son Theodore from 1916 until 1934, and from 1929 Theodore's wife Ruth lived there as well. What follows is a description of the house as they knew it.

The Exterior

The Emil Bach House is a two-story, single-family home with a basement that has a rectangular footprint and measures forty-one feet from side to side and fifty-two feet from back to front. The home sits on a cement base, and Wright used a cream-colored brick on the first floor and a grayish-colored stucco with contrasting dark brown wooden trim across the second floor. The roof is a plain flat slab rather than the Prairie-style hip roof. The flat roof contributes to the compact and solid feel of the house's exterior. The Prairie-style features of the exterior include art glass windows, wood trim, and the second floor has a triple cantilevered system of the balconies, trellises, and roof. The first floor is heavy and cubic while the second floor has a lightness derived from the wooden trellis. Wright chose to construct the home without using bricks from the Bach Brick Company—he didn't care for the reddish color of the Bach Company bricks. The bricks likely came from Ohio.

Wright broke apart the box by projecting the living room beyond the core of the cube. The first floor is protected by four fortress-like brick columns, and between these pillars are small single-pane casement windows. These windows are set deep into the columns to preserve some privacy from the busy street. The closed solid brick corners of the first floor protect the house from the urban surroundings. The house sits on a bit of a rise and fronts Sheridan

Road, which was a busy and noisy thoroughfare even in 1915. The second story's elevation places it high above the street, thus offering more privacy.

Wright concealed the front door, requiring anyone who entered the house to walk a "path of discovery" to find the way in. The path begins out on the public sidewalk at today's gated entrance to the property; from the sidewalk to the front door, which faces the rear of the home, we must make five turns while traversing the short but wandering walkway.

Courtesy of TAWANI Enterprises

Exterior of the Bach House

The east side of the home faces Lake Michigan and has an open sun porch on the second floor and a screened porch just below. These outdoor living spaces originally had a clear view of Lake Michigan. The Farcroft Apartments, built in 1928 to the northeast of the house, tower over the house and completely block the view of the lake from the terrace in that direction. The H.L. Hollister mansion, which was on Bryan Street (now Jarvis Street), was located to the southeast of the property. This property was sold to a developer in the late 1920s and was demolished to make room for the two four-story courtyard apartment buildings. The construction of these three apartment buildings spoiled the Bachs' view of the lake.

The Basement

One unusual feature of the house is its basement. Wright commonly used a design feature called a water table on which to set his Prairie houses. A water table is defined as a "structural member placed so as to divert rainwater from a building."[17] He didn't generally believe in basements, saying that "basements are damp and they're for moles. People store things there and never use them."[18] A prominent example of this water table design can be found in Wright's 1902 Arthur B. Heurtley House in Oak Park.

Arthur B. Heurtley House, Oak Park, Illinois

There are two possible reasons the Bach House has a basement. First, the compact design calls for a space below the first floor where the equipment for heating the home and for doing laundry would be located. Second, we find another link to the Fireproof House article, where Wright stated that "This house is designed with no attic, but includes 'a dry, well-lighted basement storeroom.'" Two modern-day photos of the house basement on the following page show an area that has not changed much over the past 100 years.

The First Floor

The cream-colored brick that Wright chose for both the exterior of the home and the fireplace structure provides continuity between the home's interior and exterior. The first floor encircles the central core of the chimney. Wright

Courtesy of TAWANI Enterprises

Courtesy of TAWANI Enterprises

Bach House basement

sent us on a path of discovery with the exterior of the home, and he demands we use our senses to determine which way to go to discover the interior of the home. We were wound up to the front door, and as we enter the home, we find ourselves being uncoiled into the living spaces. From the front door we turn to our right and ascend the few steps from the entry door up into the house; at the landing we immediately need to turn again to make our way toward the bookcase that is decorated with an art glass screen. The interior space is set into motion by the original concrete slab fireplace lintel, which Wright designed with a "Z" pattern. This sculpture pushes our eyes into the rest of the home. The pattern draws you from the living room around to your right into the dining area and then further to your right into the kitchen. Wright also uses bricks from the home's façade and chimney assembly to create an interesting feature in the inglenook: inverted bricks bordered by a concrete ribbon simulating a carpet in front of the fireplace.

Wright provided the home with birch wood flooring, which is very durable, and the natural color of the wood contains interesting highlights. The flooring contrasts well with the rest of the woodwork inside the house, which is unstained walnut. The strong geometric lines of the interior wall trim complement the exterior trellis design. When Emil and Anna Bach entered the home, they found the walls finished with a pebble-and-sand plaster material that was painted a creamy yellow color that Wright had custom-mixed for the home, and he called it "Sunshine."

The rooms on the first floor appear to be larger than they are because Wright used a visual trick to create this impression. There is a walnut trim board placed just at the top of the window line, which encircles the entire space. Below this trim line, the walls are painted with Wright's custom Sunshine yellow color, but above the trim board the unpainted plaster finish of the wall merges into the ceiling, giving the feeling of a larger space. The solid brick exterior walls of the first floor provide a quiet and serene living space. The first-floor casement windows have a moderate art glass design. Even though the windows are set deep into the front pillars, they offer the homeowner a pleasant view of the front yard and adjoining street. Wright added an interior flower box bordering the front windows behind the built-in couch so that a natural element could be displayed in this seating area. The modern presentation includes a straw grass display to supply this environmental feature.

Living room bench

The dining area is separated from the kitchen by a pair of swinging doors. The original kitchen had walnut cabinets, a large sink, a stove, and an icebox. From the east side of the kitchen, one can travel down a short stairway that leads to the service entrance. As the stairs descend into the basement, there is a small closet at the landing before the stairs turn and continue to descend. Emil and Anna had a summer kitchen in the basement; the coal bin and furnace were found there as well. If you exit the kitchen and bypass the stairs to the service entrance, you will find yourself at the second-floor staircase, which is placed just before the landing where you originally entered the home.

The Furnishings

From early in Wright's career, through his Prairie School period and into the Usonian era, his homes included built-in furniture as a critical part of his designs. In his Prairie-style houses, Wright often used his ability to create spaces without walls, using strategically placed pieces of built-in furniture as a design element to form these spaces. Wright's buildings were designed to be harmonious inside and out. He once said, "...it's quite impossible to consider the building as one thing, its furnishings another, and its setting and environment still another."[19]

The furniture Wright designed for the Bach House was created to be one with the building. The built-in pieces are multipurpose, allowing Wright to control the space—he as the architect decides where and how you'll sit or traverse from one room to another, with the furniture defining each space. Wright has freed his client from having to spend additional funds on furnishings by taking that chore from them. There are two unique pieces of built-in furniture on either side of the fireplace that create the inglenook: the dining/buffet table is to the left of the fireplace, and a bookcase with a built-in bench is to the right. The bookcase acts as a sentry, providing security to the interior of the home by creating a boundary between the entryway and the private areas of the house. The dining table creates a separation from the inglenook and the living room, and it includes storage cabinets in the structural design. There are also open storage cases at the ends of the built-in couch and another tall open case to the left of the kitchen entryway for storage or displaying decorative objects. The built-in furniture pieces with storage compartments limit the need for additional cabinetry elsewhere. An armoire, china cabinet, or hutch would only clutter the limited space, and any additional furniture pieces would have been an expensive luxury for the cost-conscious Bachs.

The lamp pictured here was a piece that Emil and Anna had owned while they lived in the home, and it has been handed down to their grandson Owen Bach.[20]

Courtesy of TAWANI Enterprises

Bach family lamp

The Second Floor

The stairs to the second floor face east and rise to a small landing where they turn back upon themselves and continue up to the west. At the intermediate landing there is a set of French doors which lead out and up to the sun porch, which looks out over the backyard. After ascending the stairs and arriving at the second-floor bedroom corridor, the Bachs would have found the master bedroom door to their left and slightly in front of them, their son's room to the right, and a guest bedroom further to their left. The maid's room was directly to their left and the bathroom directly to their right. Wright used another one of his favorite ploys to create movement from the second-floor corridor; he lowered the ceiling in this area. By condensing this space, he created a feeling of compression causing one to subconsciously feel the need to move from the landing into one of the nearby rooms. Wright used the same Sunshine yellow color treatment on the walls of the second floor; the trim board above the windows is also present. To create the feeling of larger bedrooms, the walls above the trim board also merge into the ceilings as they do on the first floor. This space, along with the ceiling, is unpainted plaster. When we enter these rooms, we feel released by the visual effect of expanding space.

The bedrooms each host a small private outdoor porch, and these rooms each have a set of six windows arranged in spaces that are cantilevered over the first-floor walls. Four of the windows are banded together and have a "plane" design: a large field of clear glass in the center of the window that is bordered by individual pieces of rectangular glass.

There are also two highly detailed art glass windows in each bedroom. These windows include stylized natural elements of green squares, orange triangles, white rectangles, and several pieces of clear glass that include a combination of squares and rectangles. Wright did not name the windows, nor did he leave any documentation as to what the origins of the design were, so speculation as to what his inspiration was is pointless. The maid's room did not have a balcony and only included two plain glass windows. However, this room would have had a clear view of Lake Michigan. The family's bedrooms each have small closets, and the master bedroom and the guest room have built-in dressers. Theodore's room had a built-in desk and a small built-in bookshelf. This chair pictured here is said to have come from Theodore's room and was made from the same walnut wood as the original trim in the home.[21]

Courtesy of Owen Bach family

Theodore Bach's chair

Courtesy of Owen Bach family

Theodore Bach

The Bachs' new house became for them a home of beauty and comfort. Theodore enjoyed swimming in Lake Michigan, and he looks extremely happy in this undated photo of himself—possibly a high school graduation photo—in front of the family home.

Prior to the collapse of the brickyard business around 1937 due to financial pressures caused by the Great Depression, the Bach family had prospered. Emil had become a patron of the arts and was named a Life Member of the Art Institute of Chicago in 1925. Perhaps Emil Bach's desire to support the Art Institute was inspired by his experience of living in a home that was itself a work of art.

CHAPTER SIX
Elements of Japanese Architecture in The Bach House

When the Bachs moved in to their "Little Dream House," they may not have realized the many features Wright used in their home that were derived from Japanese architecture. Three significant events occurred during Wright's lifetime that, each in its own way, must have ignited his interest in the Japanese style: the Philadelphia Centennial Exposition of 1876, Wright's employment by Joseph Lyman Silsbee in 1887, and the World's Columbian Exposition held in Chicago in 1893.

The Philadelphia Centennial Exposition

Prior to 1853, Japan was a closed society. In that year the president of the United States, Millard Fillmore, sent the naval officer Commodore Matthew Perry and four United States Navy ships to Japan to request that the Japanese open their ports for trade and diplomatic relations with the United States. By March of 1854 Japan and the United States had signed the Treaty of Kanagawa. This treaty did not make the US a full trade partner

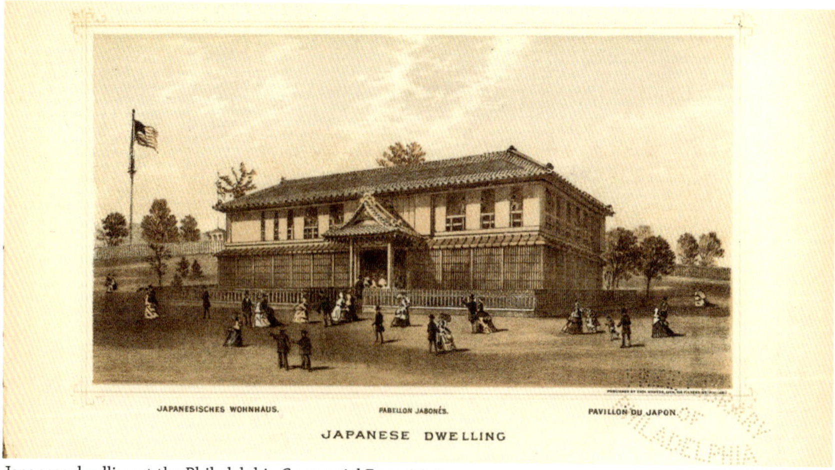

From "Centennial Portfolio by Thompson Westcott, 1876
Print and Picture Collection, Free Library of Philadelphia / Bridgeman Images

Japanese dwelling at the Philadelphia Centennial Exposition

with Japan, but it did mark the beginning of normalized relations between the two countries, which eventually led to the opening of Japan to the West.

The directors of the Centennial Commission for the Philadelphia Centennial Exposition of 1876 invited thirty-four nations, including Japan, to participate. This was one of the first public displays of Japanese art and architecture in the United States. Frank Lloyd Wright's mother, Anna, attended the exposition and purchased a set of Froebel blocks for her nine-year-old son Frank while there. Whether she also brought home books or pamphlets about Japanese culture, the Japanese buildings that were on display, or even artwork she must have seen, we will likely never know for sure, but material from this exposition may have been Frank Lloyd Wright's first exposure to Japanese culture.

Joseph Lyman Silsbee

Joseph Lyman Silsbee's influence on Wright's interest in Japanese art can't be understated. Silsbee was an amateur collector of Japanese art and displayed pieces from his collection in his home and office. Frank Lloyd Wright worked at Silsbee's office in 1887.[22]

Silsbee was also the first cousin to Ernest Francisco Fenollosa, one of the leading experts on Japanese art and culture in the United States at that time.

Fenollosa, from Boston, Massachusetts, had lived and worked in Japan from 1878 until 1890, when he became the curator of Oriental Art at the Museum of Fine Arts in Boston. While living in Boston, he was a neighbor to Edward Morse, the author of the 1886 book *Japanese Homes and their Surroundings*,

Courtesy of Christopher Payne

Joseph Lyman Silsbee

Freer and Sackler Archives / Smithsonian Institution FSA.A.01.12.03.02

Ernest Francisco Fenollosa

Collections of Maine Historical Society

Edward Morse

and the two were close friends. Morse had also lived and worked in Japan during the 1870s and was on staff at the Museum of Fine Arts in Boston in the 1890s.

Wright's association with Silsbee exposed him to Japanese art prints and to the work of Fenollosa and Morse, who both had written extensively on Japan and experienced Japanese culture firsthand while living there. Wright certainly would have been intrigued by these men and their work.

Researchers have not been able to confirm whether Wright ever met Fenollosa or Morse, but he surely would have shared their views on the beauty and importance of Japanese art prints. It's quite possible that Wright obtained some of the first Japanese woodblock prints he purchased in the United States from the collection of Fenollosa.

In 1917, Wright recalled, "When I first saw a fine print about twenty-five years ago it was an intoxicating thing. At that time Ernest Fenollosa was doing his best to persuade the Japanese people not to wantonly destroy their works of art… Fenollosa, the American, did more than anyone else to stem the tide of this folly. On one of his journeys home he brought many beautiful prints, those I made mine were the narrow tall decorative form *hashirakake*…"[23]

World's Columbian Exposition

The World's Columbian Exposition was held in Chicago in 1893. Wright was working for the firm of Adler and Sullivan at the time, and he assisted Sullivan in designing the fair's Transportation Building.

Fifty different nations, including Japan, had exhibits at the exposition. The Japanese exhibit included the Ho-o-den building, which was designed to express the Japanese culture.

The display included three structures that were connected by a sheltered walkway. The construction of the buildings was as much a part of the display as the artwork inside each building. The carpentry styles used for these buildings was typical of Japanese principles from early in the country's history. Japanese artwork in the form of scrolls, vases, and other decorative items were on display. This display at the exhibition "was to prove a watershed

Transportation Building

in Wright's personal relationship with Japan, not only apparently providing him with his first direct experience of Japanese buildings but also bringing to Chicago several of America's leading authorities on Japanese art, including Ernest Francisco Fenollosa and Edward Morse."[24]

The Columbian Exposition was where Wright had his first physical contact with the Ho-o-den on Wooded Island. Below is the plan of the Ho-o-den from the exhibition.

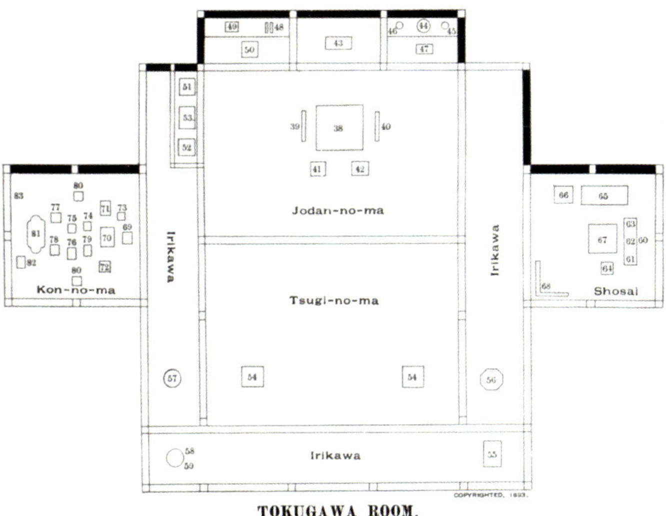

Ho-o-den floor plan

The following diagram is the plan sheet from the first-floor plan of the Bach House. The house has a study, a small seating area in front of the inglenook, a formal living room, a kitchen and dining area, and a walkway around the edge—all features that were found in the Wooded Island's Ho-o-den.

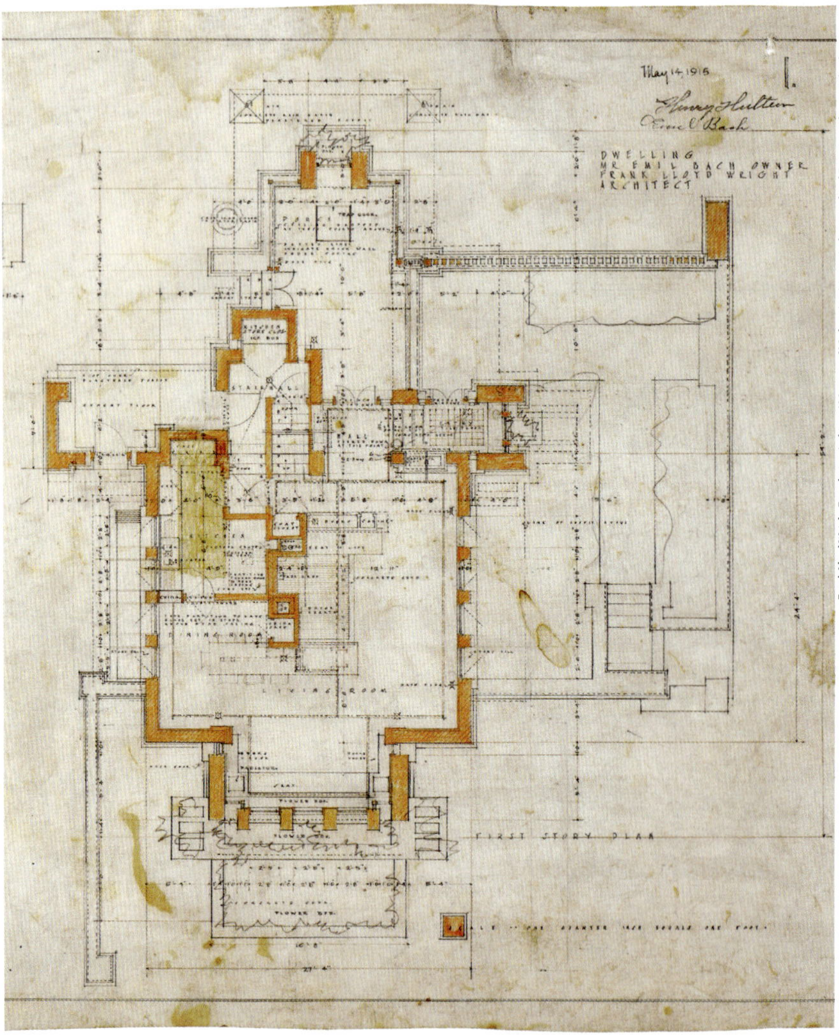

Frank Lloyd Wright Foundation Archives / Museum of Modern Art / Avery Architectural and Fine Arts Library, Columbia University

Bach House first floor plan

Besides these major elements, there are several other features of Japanese architecture that can be found in and around the house.

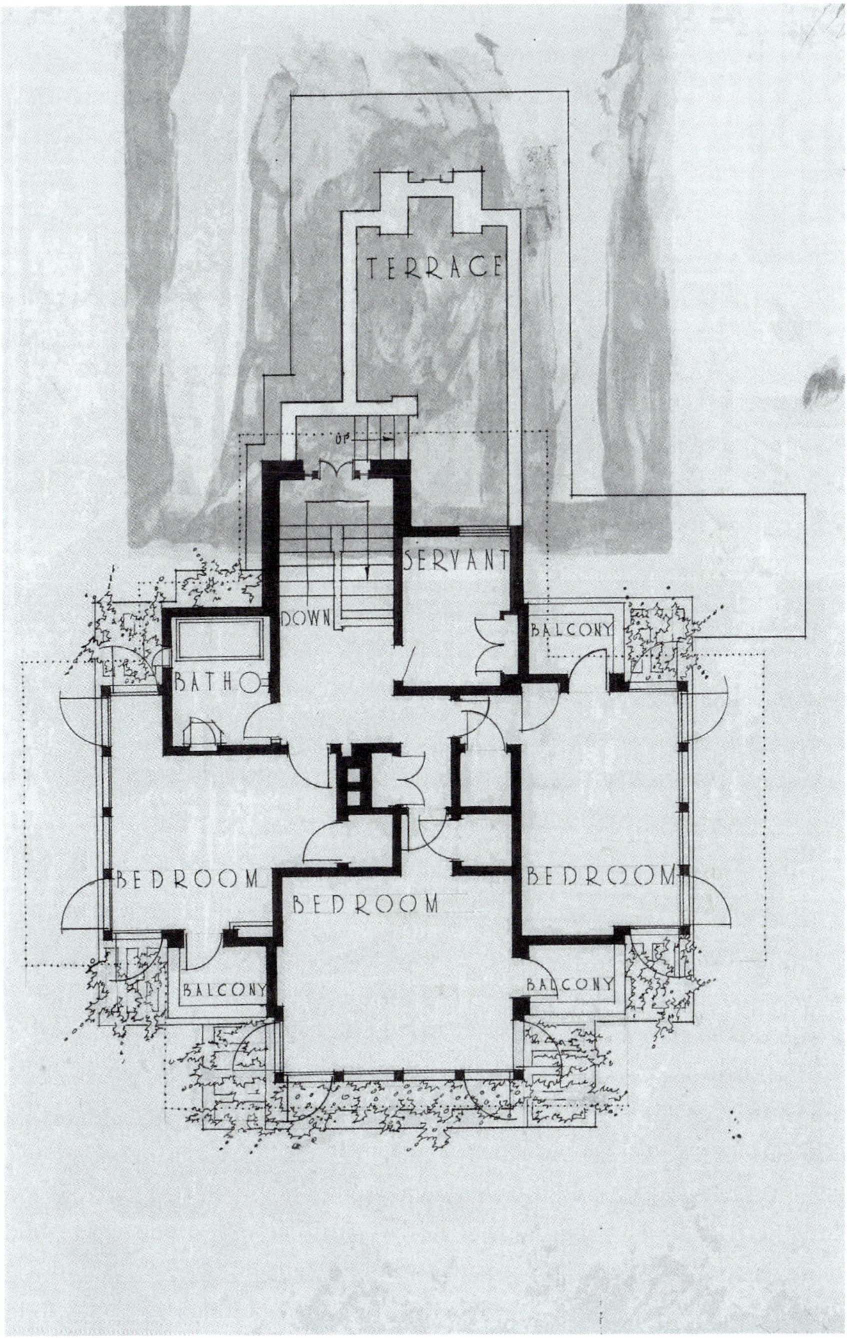

Bach House second floor plan

The Exterior

The exterior of the home as seen on Wright's plan shows his traditional path of discovery, which begins at the sidewalk and ends at the rear-facing front door. The visitor is sent on a twisting and turning path that increases in elevation and heightens the sense of discovery on this search for the home's entrance. A Japanese home often has a zig-zag entryway, with this design serving two purposes: to "throw evil spirits off one's path" and to increase the apparent separation of the domains on either side of the stagger.[25] The raised and circuitous walkway of the house is quite visible in this undated but early photograph taken by Walter Burley Griffin.

National Library of Australia, PIC/9929/1511

Exterior walkway

In a Japanese home the fence, or *tamagaki*, can be made from different types of natural materials. In Wright's Bach House, the rear of the garden court is separated from the backyard by a fence made from brick and rough-cut wood. The wooded square windows are also like portholes to the rear yard.

His imagination sparked by the Japanese art prints he had been collecting, Wright traveled with his wife Catherine and their friends Cecilia and Ward Willits to Japan in 1905, just four years after Wright had designed their Prairie-style home in the fashionable North Shore suburb of Highland Park.

Courtesy of TAWANI Enterprises

Bach House porthole fence

Over a period of three months, the Wrights and the Willitses explored ten different Japanese cities after landing in Yokohama Harbor on March 7.[26]

As Wright and his companions traveled, he photographed many different buildings and various landscaped vistas. Upon his return home, he created a photo album for himself, perhaps to look back at and remember his trip, or possibly to reignite his imagination. During their time in Japan, the party toured several castles and temples, including the Nijo-jo Castle. Seen below is

Courtesy of Eric Obershaw

A Japanese castle featuring a *yagura* (turret) and a *kirikomihagi* wall a *yagura*, (a tower or turret), which is on the southeast corner of the castle's property. The *yagura* has a double-hipped roof and a *kirikomihagi* wall below.

This style of wall uses stones that have been fashioned so that each piece can be mounted upon the previous layer, allowing the edges of the neighboring stone to align and create a fortification to guard the castle and the nobility who lived there.

The Bach House has two protective brick walls, one on the north side of the building and another to the south side. These walls do not need to provide the same type of protection as the walls of Nijo-jo Castle, but they are reminiscent of these fortifications.

Courtesy of TAWANI Enterprises

Protective brick walls

The Outdoor Living Spaces

The rear of the house has two outdoor areas. The first floor has an *engawa*-like porch, or veranda, which creates a transitional space between the interior of the house the gardens. The second area is the sun porch located directly above the *engawa*. In a traditional Japanese home the *engawa* would be a covered transitional space, meaning that one could easily pass from outside the home to inside and back again. This area would have seating and a view of the ever-present gardens. The *engawa* could be open or include shutters for protection from the weather. Through a set of French doors situated just off the entryway landing, one can easily walk into a protected screened-in porch where outdoor furniture would be placed.

The view from the *engawa* opens out onto the backyard gardens to the east, and to the south the terrace garden can be seen. There is another French door facing west to allow you to walk down a few steps into the rear yard to experience the gardens first hand. Even in winter, the rear yard offers a serene experience.

Courtesy of TAWANI Enterprises

Bach House rear yard

The Tea House

The *chashitsu*, or tea house, is a separate piece of Japanese architecture found on the Bach House property. This space is designed to be used for tea ceremonies or other gatherings. The tea house, which was not designed by Wright, was added to the site in 2008 under the ownership of Jane Feerer, but it is a lovely space to sit and meditate or gather with friends.

The Interior

After traveling the home's entrance path, you find yourself at the formal entryway, which is set in the style of a Japanese *genkan*. In a Japanese home, the *genkan* would be at the main entryway of the home but at a lower level

Tea house, interior

Tea house, exterior

Courtesy of TAWANI Enterprises

Genkan (main entryway)

than the main floor. In this alcove homeowners may store shoes and coats, but more importantly the space provides some security to the home. When callers would arrive they would be greeted by servants and vetted before being allowed to enter the family's secure spaces.

The front door is open to the courtyard outside and there are three steps that lead up to the main living area of the home. This space includes durable clay tiles and views to the outdoor gardens.

On the landing at top of the entryway stairs we find three architectural elements often found in a Japanese home: the *kamoi*, the *ramma*, and the *tokonoma*.

In the rooms of a Japanese home, a horizontal timber rail called a *kamoi* is installed at the top of a door header, and the rail travels around the room to create a separation between the lower walls and ceiling. With a change in color from darker below the *kamoi* to lighter above, the room seems to expand. A *kamoi* was used in the Ho-o-den at World's Columbian Exposition. In the Bach House, Wright uses this same feature, as seen here at the landing and in the subsequent photograph of the living room as well.

Courtesy of TAWANI Enterprises

Bach House stair landing. Note the *kamoi* (wood rail) along top, *ramma* (wood slats) below the *kamoi*, and *tokonoma* (alcove) displaying art below the *ramma*

The wood slat, grill-like feature in a Japanese home is called a *ramma*, which is similar to a transom. This feature is an open ventilating fretwork, and here it is installed just below the *kamoi*. This grill allows for air flow between the upper and lower floors of the home. In a Japanese home, the *ramma* is often a carved image.

At the top of the entryway stairs and below the *ramma* is a feature called a *tokonoma*. As Wright describes it in his autobiography: "...they always have a little recess...devoted only to fine arts...they call this treasure alcove the

Courtesy of TAWANI Enterprises

Living room. Note the *kamoi* above the Sunshine yellow wall.

tokonoma."[27] An item often found in a *tokonoma* would be a Japanese scroll called a *kakemono*.

Once in the house, as you turn from the entryway landing, you are confronted with a bookcase and must move around it to gain entry to the rest of the house. The bookcase includes a pillowed bench along the back side. The area is bordered on three sides by the bench, the fireplace, and the buffet table forming the inglenook. In a Japanese home, this area could be considered the *shosai*, or study.

Across from the inglenook is another sitting area where the family can meet with friends and entertain guests—the *jodannoma*. In the Ho-o-den from the Columbian Exposition, the *jodannoma* was a private sitting area separated by a change in elevation from the area where guests were greeted. In the Bach House, Wright transforms the *jodannoma* into an open seating area across from the inglenook.

The next typical Japanese feature Wright used in the Bach House is the *irikawa*, a walkway on the periphery of a room that allows a person to pass from

Above: jodannoma (sitting area). *Below: irikawa* (walkway)

one room to the next. To travel from the inglenook to the primary living room, one must pass through an *irikawa*-like corridor.

The *konnoma*, or dining area, is between the living room and the *daidokoro*, or kitchen. Wright designed a simple glass and wood transom to be placed above the kitchen door.

Courtesy of TAWANI Enterprises

Konnoma (dining area)

THE SECOND FLOOR

Often Japanese rooms were designed to be multi-functional, so a Japanese bedroom was a bedroom only by night. The bedrooms were designed simply and furnished with *tatami* floor mats.

The second-floor bedrooms in the Bach House are traditional American-style bedrooms, but in each room Wright included at least one piece of built-in furniture. These pieces would be called *tsuke-shoin* in a Japanese home.

Courtesy of TAWANI Enterprises

The guest bedroom includes a built-in makeup table and a chair, the master bedroom has a built-in dresser, and the child's room has a small built-in desk. All of these pieces are reproductions of the ones Wright designed for the house.

Courtesy of TAWANI Enterprises

Previous page: built-in makeup table in guest bedroom

Top: built-in dresser in master bedroom

Right: built-in desk in child's room

Courtesy of TAWANI Enterprises

The architectural influences from Japanese homes can be found in Frank Lloyd Wright's designs from as early as the 1896 Isidore Heller House.

A interior photo of the Heller House shows a view of the main hallway. The hall like the *irikawa* corridor unites the dining room and living room at opposing ends. The hall also provides access into the reading room and reception hall to the right and the second floor stairway to the left. In the Heller House, Wright places the *ramma* ventilating slats above the staircase to provide air flow between the two levels of the home. This location also allows light from the floor above to enter the stairway below.

Historic American Buildings Survey / Library of Congress

Irikawa (walkway) of the Isidore Heller House (1896)

The 1915 Emil Bach House continued Wright's tradition of using elements from Japanese architecture in his American homes. The character of the Japanese art prints and the architecture of Japan would continue to be represented in Wright's building designs throughout his career.

CHAPTER SEVEN
A Brief History of Bach House Ownership

WITH THE GREAT DEPRESSION TAKING a toll on the Bach Brick Company, Emil and Anna Bach decided to sell their home in 1934 to Joseph and Florence Peacock for $14,500. After the company closed its doors around 1937, Emil and Anna relocated to California, where Anna's family lived. Their son Theodore and his wife, Ruth, moved to Rockford, Illinois.

The Peacocks sold the home to the James family in 1947, and in that same year the Jameses sold the home to Manuel and Ridi Spiesman. The Spiesmans later divorced and sold the property to Manuel and Lillian Weiss in 1951. Upon Frank Lloyd Wright's death in 1959, the Chicago newspapers were filled with photographs of his various buildings in the area. Weiss was still living in the Bach House at that time and was interviewed by the *Chicago Sun-Times*, saying, "Even though Mr. Wright designed the house in 1915, it has all the features of contemporary houses. Our eight years here have been delightful."[28]

The Weisses sold the property to James Blinder in June of 1959. Four years later, Blinder purchased the home at 4709 Sheridan, which was the neighboring property to the south. He subsequently had this house torn down to create one large lot. Blinder sold the Bach House and the adjoining vacant lot in 1970 to the Blinder Building Corporation, which was owned by his father.[29] In July of 1970, Frank and Carol Miller purchased the house and the adjoining lot for $100,000. The sale was financed by the Blinder Building Corporation, who continued to hold the mortgage on the properties. This type of real estate transaction would have been beneficial to both parties as the Blinder Building Corporation would be earning interest on the deal, and the Millers would not need to pay bank fees or traditional closing costs.

By 1975 only Mr. Miller and his six-year-old son Frank, Jr. remained living in the house and Mr. Miller though it was too large for them, so he decided to sell the home. Previously Miller had agreed to the City of Chicago's request to landmark the house, which would prevent alterations or demolition without city permission. This move by Miller was rather unusual; homeowners usually resist having their properties landmarked because of the restrictive nature of these designations. The Bach House and the vacant lot next door are both zoned RT-4, which in Chicago would permit a high-rise residential building to be constructed there. Miller could have made a considerable profit by selling the house and vacant lot to a developer who likely would have torn down the house to make way for an apartment tower. However, when Miller was interviewed about the possible sale of his home to a developer he said, "That's exactly what I'm not going to do." [30]

Instead, Miller sold the properties to two physicians, Fedor and Sirirat Banuchi, for $130,000 in 1978. In 1983 the Banuchis donated a preservation easement on both the exterior and interior of the Bach House to the Landmarks Preservation Council of Illinois (LPCI). This type of easement prohibits the destruction or alteration of the house without approval from the City of Chicago and LPCI.

The Bach House went on the market again in 1998. Originally, the house itself was listed for $600,000, but in January 2000, the Banuchis agreed to sell the house for $437,500 and the adjacent vacant lot, which had been separately listed, for $240,000. The house and adjoining lot were sold to a LaSalle Bank trust that was owned by Chicago businessman Reza Toulabi.

Toulabi put the house and adjacent lot up for sale for $2.5 million in 2003;. The listing was later reduced to $1.9 million, but a buyer still could not be found. It is likely that potential buyers shied away from purchasing the home because of its landmark status and the preservation easement, which would limit any physical alterations to the building. Surely another concern would have been the home's location on Sheridan Road, a busy thoroughfare connecting Chicago and its suburbs to the north. There were no interested buyers for the house between 2003 and 2005, even at the reduced asking price.

Toulabi finally decided to try to sell the house and neighboring lot via an auction in March of 2005, with a reserve price of $750,000.

This was not the first time a Wright home had been sold at auction. In Cincinnati, Ohio, in 2003, the owner of a Wright-designed Usonian house dating from 1954 said, "Perhaps in an auction, it will find its own price." [31]

At the time of the auction, both the house and the adjoining lot were sold together. One advertisement for the auction stated certain advantages of this: "An expansive 45-by-150-foot lawn immediately to the south of the house, zoned RT-4, allows bidders the option of new development. Potential uses for the lot include detached houses, two-flats, townhouses, and low density, multi-family residential buildings." [32]

Courtesy of TAWANI Enterprises

The Bach House to the left and the vacant lot to the right, 2005

The bidding on the home opened at $750,000, and after a few minutes and a few bid submittals, Jane Feerer purchased the Emil Bach House. [33]

The auction price for the home had been reported as $1.17 million, or $420,000 above the opening bid. Feerer's intentions for the house were to make it her home and restore as many of the original Wright-designed elements as possible. She also intended to preserve the vacant lot to the south as an open yard. In October of 2010 she transferred the ownership to Jennifer Pritzker, president and CEO of TAWANI Enterprises.

The Bach House has had twelve owners from 1915 through 2010. Many of these owners spoke of how they enjoyed their time living there.

In a letter from Anna Bach to Frank Lloyd Wright on November 15, 1956, she described her home as "not only a livable house but a lovable home." In a second letter from Anna Bach written in 1961 to James Blinder, Anna refers to her former home as "...a thing of beauty."

In 1975 Frank Miller was quoted in the *Chicago Tribune* as saying "...it's a great family house, and you don't have to treat it like a museum to enjoy it."

In a conversation with the author in 2016, Feerer said, "I loved how enfolding the house was, and when the sun streamed into the house from the east in the morning, it set all the rooms aglow with the paint color we so carefully matched to original paint chips we found during demolition of some walls. Early mornings were always delightful."

When asked what her favorite room in the house was, Pritzker said, "My favorite room at the Emil Bach House is the living room. It's comfortable, cozy and people don't have to be nervous sitting on the furniture. It's great for entertaining or relaxing. You can sit back and read, surf the web or write or just enjoy the view from the room. I also like the rich brown satin of the woodwork."

CHAPTER EIGHT
The Bach House Achieves Local and National Recognition

DURING THE 1970S, CHICAGO OFFICIALS were searching for ways to reverse the effects of the economic decline caused by high unemployment and inflation rates. Neighborhoods were in decline from decreasing population and falling real estate values. Rather than building new homes, federal, state, and local officials were encouraging the preservation of existing properties.

The Commission on Chicago Landmarks began looking for ways to encourage economic growth by conferring landmark status on significant buildings or districts within the City. The Commission found a perfect opportunity on Sheridan Road in Rogers Park.

A Chicago Landmark

The Emil Bach House was designated a Chicago landmark on September 28, 1977.[34] However, the story of how the house became a Chicago landmark actually began in August of 1973, when David Hanks, the chairman of the Advisory Committee on Architecture of Chicago, wrote a letter to Samuel Lichtman, the chairman of the Commission on Chicago Historical and Architectural Landmarks (CCHAL), urging the Commission to consider landmark status for the house. There are two points in this letter that demonstrate the need for urgency. The first statement asserts that the "Bach House is one of a handful of Wright's houses left standing within the city. It is necessary that these few remaining examples be preserved."

The second statement is attributed to Chicago Landmarks Commission member Robert Shelby, who said, "Many Sheridan Road Wright houses have been lost to the pressures of real estate values." He is likely referring to the loss of the Oscar M. Steffens House, which had been demolished in 1963, and possibly the L. K. Horner House, demolished in 1952.

At the July 1, 1974 meeting of the CCHAL, a vote was held on a resolution proposing that the Commission's recommendation to designate the Bach House as a Chicago landmark be forwarded to the city's Department of Development and Planning (DDP) for their further recommendation; this resolution passed unanimously. In August of 1974 the DDP issued a fairly comprehensive report to establish their recommendation to designate the house as a Chicago landmark. The report stated that such a designation would have a positive effect on the immediate neighborhood. It was recommended that the adjacent lot, at 7409 N. Sheridan, though not part of the original site, should be included in the designation.

Part of the process of considering the house for landmark status was to determine who actually owned the home. In 1974 the Commission had assumed that it was owned by the Blinder Building Corporation, but the owner was Frank Miller, who had purchased the home from the company in July 1970. At the May 26, 1977 meeting of the CCHAL, Miller testified that he was in fact the owner of the property and that the Blinder Building Corporation held the mortgage. After determining ownership of the property, the Commission needed the consent of Miller to secure the landmark designation. In its initial letter requesting this consent, the Commission cited these five criteria that the Emil Bach House met for consideration for landmark status:

1. *Its character, interest or value as part of the development, heritage or cultural characteristics of the City of Chicago, State of Illinois, or the United States*
2. *Its embodiment of distinguishing characteristics of an architectural type or specimen*
3. *Its identification as the work of an architect or master builder whose individual work has influenced the development of the City of Chicago*
4. *Its embodiment of elements of architectural design, detail, materials, or craftsmanship which represent a significant an architectural innovation*

5. *Its unique location or singular physical characteristic representing an established and familiar visual features of a neighborhood, community, or the City of Chicago*

After some ongoing correspondence between the Commission and Miller, he granted his consent in April of 1975. In May of 1977, the Commission held its final hearing on the landmark designation of the house, during which many of the attributes and characteristics of the home were restated. It was also during this hearing that Miller requested the vacant lot be removed from the landmark designation, with this request being approved in June of 1977. The Committee, having reviewed all the testimony given at the hearing, forwarded its recommendation to the full Chicago City Council for review and approval at its September 28, 1977 meeting. The City Council voted in favor of the designation and the Emil Bach House received landmark status at that time.

Emil Bach House

7415 North Sheridan Road

Designated as a Chicago Landmark
by the City Council of Chicago
on September 28, 1977

Designation as a Chicago Landmark is a great honor, indicating that a structure, area, or object is important to Chicago and in some way symbolizes the city's history, its spirit, or its achievements. A bronze plaque, commemorating this designation and installed at the landmark, states:

> One of the last of Wright's small urban houses, the Bach House combines elements of the Prairie style with a compact plan well suited for an interior lot. The inward orientation of the house ensures the privacy of its residents and reflects Wright's idea of the importance of family life.

Ceremonies observing the installation of the bronze plaque occurred on this eighth day of May, 1978, in Preston Bradley Hall of The Chicago Public Library Cultural Center.

John C. Marcin
City Clerk

Michael A. Bilandic
Mayor of the City of Chicago

Edwin P. Fifielski
Chairman, City Council Committee on Cultural and Economic Development

Ira J. Bach
Secretary and Acting Chairman, Commission on Chicago Historical and Architectural Landmarks

Bach House Chicago Landmark certificate

City of Chicago Department of Planning and Development

Bach House brochure from CCHAL

A Historic Place

Following the Bach House's designation as a Chicago landmark, the building achieved national recognition in 1979 when it was placed on the National Register of Historic Places (NRHP), a program managed by the National Park Service.

In 1966, the federal government passed the National Historic Preservation Act, leading to the creation of the Illinois Historic Site Survey. Historic surveys would focus on the architectural, historic, or archaeological value of the site. Funding for these survey projects could come from any combination of federal, state, or private resources.

The architectural survey was completed under the direction of Dr. Paul Sprague, a faculty member of the Department of Art History at the University of Chicago in the spring of 1976.[35] Students from Sprague's architectural studies class completed applications for eight properties throughout the state of Illinois for placement on the National Register of Historic Places. These eight applications, including one for the Bach House, were submitted to the Illinois Historic Sites Advisory Council, a body which makes recommendations for the NRHP. The recommendation was made, and final approval of the application was received from the Illinois Department of Conservation (IDC) in January 1977. From there it was submitted to the National Park Service office in Washington, DC.

On December 26, 1978, Keith Sculle, the National Register coordinator for the IDC, provided a letter to William Murtagh, Keeper of the Register, and to William Brabham of the National Park Service with responses and clarifications. Ultimately, the Emil Bach House was entered into the National Registry of Historical Places on January 23, 1979.

The Bach House's designation as a Chicago landmark, its listing on the registry of National Historical Places, and the Landmarks Preservation Council of Illinois easement granted by the Banuchi family in 1983 have certainly helped save the building from the wrecking ball. Perhaps the landmark designation in 1977 didn't spur economic development at that time, but now, after the home's restoration and use as a tourist site and vacation rental, this type of change is happening in Rogers Park.

Opposite page: Quotation is from correspondence from Frank Lloyd Wright to Anna Bach, January 1957.

PART THREE

RESTORING, PRESERVING, AND CELEBRATING THE BACH HOUSE

"Dear Mrs. Bach: Will never forget the 'Bach House' nor the Bachs. Glad you remember it all. Sincerely, Frank Lloyd Wright"

—in a letter to Anna Bach, 1957

CHAPTER NINE
Bach House Alterations, Additions, and Improvements

THERE IS LITTLE EVIDENCE OF major changes to the appearance of the Bach House between 1915 and 1945, a period that included the Great Depression and was bookended by two world wars. Americans had less disposable income; the average man's work week was eight to ten hours a day, six days a week; and televisions would not become commercially popular until after World War II. Beginning in the late 1950s, the American family style of living changed, and homes were now being built with casual family rooms or dens. The television became the focal point of these new rooms, where people could be entertained by the newest comedy or drama.

The house's compact first floor did not lend itself to creating an area for stretching out to watch TV, and eventually accommodations to a changing lifestyle were made: built-in furniture was removed to enlarge the interior spaces, and new living spaces were created by enclosing the two outdoor porch areas.

According to an interview conducted by Harboe Architects with James Blinder, who purchased the Bach House in 1959, some remodeling projects had taken place prior to his purchase. Major changes to the home included the enclosure of the first-floor porch and second-floor sun porch. The built-in furniture including the child's desk and bedroom dressers had been removed at some point. The inglenook had been dissolved by the removal of the bookcase, bench, and dining table. A new breakfast bar between the kitchen and living room had been installed, and the original art glass windows were removed. Interior surfaces which had been painted over included the plaster, the millwork, and the brick fireplace. The exterior stucco surface and the wood trellises had also been painted. A concrete ramp on the north side of the house leading to the back entry was replaced with concrete stairs.

Courtesy of TAWANI Enterprises

In the above photograph, you can see how the sun porch and lower patio deck were completely closed in at one time. You can also see that the guest bedroom's balcony door had been closed off. Also visible are a non-original patio surface at the rear of the home and non-original landscaping.

The photograph below from 1966 shows how the home looked with the inglenook eliminated. You can also see into the enclosed porch, which by then was converted into a family room.

Historic American Buildings Survey / Library of Congress

During Harboe Architects' interview with Blinder, he stated that once he had purchased the building, he began to renovate, repair, and remodel the home. He completed such critical upgrades as replacing the boiler, the electrical system, and the roof. He also completed renovations to the kitchen, bathroom, and basement. He converted the maid's second-floor bedroom into a second bathroom. Mr. Blinder also completed several cosmetic improvements, including stripping and refinishing the interior millwork, painting the exterior stucco, and cleaning the exterior brick. One of Blinder's enhancements to the site that has stood the test of time was the purchase and subsequent demolition of the building directly south of the Bach House on Sheridan Road. This lot is now part of the landscape. The removal of this building has provided the owners the luxury of being able to enjoy a park-like feature on this urban site.

To understand the other changes that were made to both the interior and exterior of the home prior to the 1970s, one needs only to review the 1966 Historic American Building Survey (HABS). According to the National Park Service's website, the HABS program is the federal government's oldest preservation program. This program is used to document the nation's most important historic sites. Often the staff from HABS work in partnership with state and local governments, private industry, professional societies, universities, preservation groups, and other federal agencies.

Alterations to the original design noted in the HABS drawings and not listed in alterations made prior to 1959 include the addition of a storage shed adjacent to the north entry gate and new stone coping on the south retaining wall. The trellis on the ground level on the west side of the house was removed. The partition and door between the kitchen and dining room was removed. An original window from the new second floor bathroom (the former maid's room) was replaced with a door that opened to the porch. The balcony on the southeast side of the house was enclosed as a closet for the guest bedroom, and a new window was added on the east wall of the second-floor bathroom.

The next series of renovations occurred between 1983 and 1999 while Fedor and Sirirat Banuchi owned the property. The Banuchis completed renovations to the kitchen. They removed the original leaded glass from the windows in the north bedroom. They fixed in place originally operable windows on the first and second floors, and they replaced much of the original plaster with drywall. They removed the glass doors, sidelights, and transom from the entry into the second-floor sun porch. They also installed a forced-air system for heating; this system would have allowed them to add an air conditioning system at that same time, though there was no evidence of an air conditioning system ever having been installed.

In 1978 the Banuchis had also considered completing a major remodeling effort that would have completely removed both the sun porch and screened porch below and replaced these structures with an addition that would have altered the look of the home. Because the home was designated as a Chicago landmark, this remodeling effort could not take place without the consent of the Commission on Chicago Landmarks. The Banuchis took several members of the commission on a tour of their home in hopes of securing their approval for the project. During this tour, these commission members provided the Banuchis with a verbal approval of their request. However, because this tour was not a properly convened commission meeting, their approval held no value. Subsequently, at its June 4, 1979 meeting, the commission voted to deny the Banuchis' request. The commission stated that "the addition to the Bach House will more than double its volume and alter forever the underlying concept and configuration for its design."

The Banuchis were no doubt upset at the commission's response, having previously received a verbal approval. Because the building had been placed on the National Register of Historic Places in January of 1979, they had to take their case to the United States Department of the Interior. The department concurred with the commission and cited in their April 9, 1980 rejection letter the following comments: "...the proposed addition as described in the submitted plans will obscure the rear elevation of the house and will greatly alter the size, scale, and character of the property."

The letter did include information on pursuing an appeal of the agency's decision, but it seems that the Banuchis chose not to follow up on this option. In 1999 they sold the property to Reza Toulabi, who subsequently sold the home to Jane Feerer in 2005.

CHAPTER TEN
Restoration of the Bach House, Phase 1

JANE FEERER FIRST BECAME INTERESTED in Frank Lloyd Wright's Prairie-style architecture when she was living in Japan. As an enthusiast of Wright's work, she would often review the buildings listed for sale on the Frank Lloyd Wright Building Conservancy webpage. In the early 2000s she was living in Chicago's Irving Park neighborhood in a traditional Chicago bungalow.

She was considering renovating this home, but she also had contemplated purchasing the Wright-designed S. A. Foster House, dated from 1900 and located in Chicago's West Pullman neighborhood.

Deborah Mercer

S. A. Foster House, Chicago, Illinois

However, when the Bach House became available, Feerer began to consider buying it. She realized that several of the features included in the building were characteristics she had wanted to include in her bungalow renovation. When the sale price for the house was lowered and the decision was made to sell the building via auction, Feerer felt that this type of purchase arrangement gave her the best opportunity to procure a Wright-designed home in Chicago.

During Feerer's tenure owning the home, she not only intended to restore the house to its original 1915 appearance but also planned to live there. She summed up her philosophy on owning a Wright property: "What is the point of owning a Frank Lloyd Wright house if it is not as close to the original configuration of the house as possible?"

After reviewing the original house drawings from the Taliesin archives, and knowing that she would be doing the restoration in stages, Feerer thought it would be quite doable. After purchasing the property, Feerer worked with her preferred contractors, Fred Harboe and Peder Dahlberg, to create a plan for the restoration. The majority of the work was completed between March of 2005 and July of 2006. She moved into the house after most of the restoration projects had been completed.

Courtesy of Jane Feerer

Pre-restoration bathroom

When Feerer bought the house, it was in a livable condition: the bathrooms worked, the appliances in the kitchen were functional, and there were no obvious structural issues.

However, the last renovations had been done in the late 1980s and early 1990s, so much of the interior design and appliances were from that period. The bathrooms had thirty-five-year-old fixtures, and the kitchen had plain stock cabinets.

Courtesy of Jane Feerer

Pre-restoration kitchen

An interesting piece of architectural history was discovered during the first phase of the restoration when the 1960s-era breakfast bar was removed. As can be seen in the photograph below, this piece of built in furniture was installed in front of the kitchen doorway between the extensions of the brick chimney and the interior north wall of the building.

© Barbara Crane

1960s-era breakfast bar

When the breakfast bar was installed, it covered an interior storage compartment that had been built into the brick chimney extension. This cabinet, shown in the black-and-white photo below, had a solid walnut wood door with a rectangular trim feature, plain hinges, and a simple brass knob. As seen in the next photograph, this cabinet is now exposed and usable. Based on tests done on this wooden cabinet door and comparisons to the original plan sheets used for the home's construction, it is believed that the cabinet door is the only piece of original walnut woodwork left in the building from 1915.

Using the rediscovered door as a template, the kitchen cabinets were restored to their original appearance as designed by Wright.

A company called Quality Finishing and Custom Cabinetry Services of Elk Grove, Illinois, was hired to do the kitchen remodeling for the first phase of

Courtesy of TAWANI Enterprises

Courtesy of TAWANI Enterprises

Left: Rediscovered cabinet door. *Right:* The same door after restoration

Courtesy of TAWANI Enterprises

The restored kitchen

the project. All the kitchen cabinets are custom-made from walnut just like the ones originally planned by Wright.

Feerer had said in a 2015 documentary about the Bach House that Frank Lloyd Wright was her restoration architect, because she was able to use the original Wright drawings from Taliesin to do the restoration work. Dahlberg also noted in the film that these plans were used for both phases of the restoration.

Owen Bach, the grandson of Emil and Anna Bach, had many historic documents pertaining to the house. He provided the original contract, which listed the material specifications that helped the restorers determine the types of finishes that would give the home the look and feel of a 1915 dwelling.

When Owen Bach and his family visited the house for the first time, prior to any of the restoration work, he brought some photos of the interior of the house. One photo showed Anna Bach sitting on the fireplace bench, and this was helpful to verify the height of the bench against the brickwork. Another photo showed the dining room table.

Courtesy of Owen Bach family

As work progressed on the restoration, Feerer discovered two major challenges she needed to resolve. The first was the cost of the project, which she addressed by stretching the restoration out over time. The second was using good contractors. Feerer stated, "As far as contractors were concerned, I had the advantage of knowing people who had been doing historic renovations for some time and who knew people involved in this type of project."

Courtesy of Owen Bach family

Top: original dining room table
Bottom: Anna Bach at the fireplace

Feerer had worked extensively with a local general contractor. The firm removed the previously installed drywall and reinstalled plaster with a finish that was period-accurate to 1915. The company was also able to re-engineer and install a birchwood floor that was similar to the original. As time went on, they also worked on repairing and/or replacing windows, doors, and interior trim. New wall sconces and light fixtures were installed;

however, given that no drawings or photographs of the 1915 originals existed, the lighting elements that were installed were a design that was sympathetic to traditional Prairie styles rather than being exact replicas.

Feerer's construction manager directed different contracting crews to complete work on the exterior of the building that included repairs to the woodwork and masonry. Crews also renovated the family bathroom to its original configuration based on original drawings from the Frank Lloyd Wright archives.

Feerer worked down the list she had originally created so she could to make the house her own. Once she moved in, the remaining projects were completed one by one.

Feerer had wanted to have a swimming pool and spa area for her personal use at her home. She felt that the area just south of where the garage stood would make a suitable location for this type of facility. Drawing on her memories of time she had spent in Japan, she sketched out the original design of what would become the tea house, and her team of architects completed the detailed building plans for the necessary permits and construction drawings. She also needed to procure the approval of the Landmarks Preservation Council of Illinois for the changes at the site, which she received in July of 2008. The Landmark Division had determined that since the garage building was "not specifically called out as a protected element" in the preservation agreement of 1983, and that since the new tea house would not be readily seen from Sheridan Road, they would have no objections to the removal of the existing garage and the installation of the proposed spa building. To make room for the tea house, a portion of the original garage was demolished. During the demolition of that structure, several original Chicago common bricks made by the Bach company were discovered. Remember John Lloyd Wright's letter to Emil Bach in 1915 telling him he could save money by building the garage at a later date, and Frank Lloyd Wright's decision not to use Bach bricks in the Bach House. The discovery of these bricks does lead one to speculate that the garage would have been constructed sometime after 1915, when the Bachs could use their own bricks.

Feerer resided in the home from 2006 until 2011 and found that there were pros and cons in living there. She loved how the sun streamed into the house in the morning, saying, "...it set all the rooms aglow with the paint color which was so carefully matched to original paint chips that were found during the demolition of some wall sections. Early mornings were always delightful." And though it seemed to some people to be a very large house for one person, the rooms were small and, she felt, perfect for her.

On the down side, Sheridan Road is a busy thoroughfare, and the noise from vehicle traffic as well as emergency vehicles that drove by at all hours of the day and night was discomforting. Feerer felt that the overhangs on both floors trapped and magnified the traffic noise, something Wright could not have foreseen. Also, before she was able to get locks on the property's gates, people who knew that the home was designed by Frank Lloyd Wright would walk onto the property and even come up to the main entry door and peer into the home.

In 2010, Feerer had the opportunity to retire from her position as Senior Vice President and Chief Financial Officer of TAWANI Enterprises. At that time she had been living in Chicago for eighteen years and she thought it would be an opportune time to seek out new experiences both professionally and personally, and so she put the Bach House up for sale. Feerer included in the sale of the building and adjoining property some pieces of furniture that she felt had become integral to the home, and since she had done extensive research on the Bach House, several documents about the history of the house including, photographs, and construction forms were included in the deal.

CHAPTER ELEVEN
Restoration of the Bach House, Phase 2

WHEN JANE FEERER MADE THE decision to sell the Bach House in 2010, she did so with the hope that the next owner would continue the work she had started. With her carefully considered choice to pass the torch to Jennifer Pritzker, we see the genesis of the restoration's second phase. An article in *Crain's Chicago Business* from December 2, 2010 stated, "Pritzker paid $1.7 million for Frank Lloyd Wright's Emil Bach House on Sheridan Road in Rogers Park, according to property records."[36]

Jennifer Pritzker has always had a keen interest in preserving historic properties. Through her company, TAWANI Enterprises, she has been involved in the restoration of the Monroe Building on Michigan Avenue in Chicago; the Lincoln Way Inn of Franklin Grove, Illinois; the Stone Terrace Bed and Breakfast in Evanston, Illinois; and the Cat's Cradle Bed and Breakfast, now the Lang House, located directly next door to the Bach House. She originally became interested in Frank Lloyd Wright's architecture when she was a child. In the mid-1950s, Pritzker's family lived next to what is now known as the Weltzheimer/Johnson House in Oberlin, Ohio. This home was designed by Wright in 1947, and it was the first Usonian house built in Ohio.

In 1992, the house was given to Oberlin College to serve as a guest house for the art department. The house is now open to the public for tours and programs. Pritzker found it gratifying that this house was available to the public. When she purchased the Bach House in 2011, she felt that the home had a significant link to the past. She planned to continue the restoration that Feerer had begun and saw the investment as an opportunity to complete an architectural restoration to a significant building from Wright's career; this was also a way to provide people with the experience of living in a Wright-designed home by creating an architecturally inspired vacation

Weltzheimer/Johnson House

rental property. Pritzker's overall goal was to restore a property that had gone through many alterations over the years but still had a certain magical quality to it. She also wanted to bring the property up to current building codes while restoring its 1915 charm and ambiance.

Pritzker believes that it is important to allow the community at large to take advantage of this historic site. By restoring the home and opening the building for rentals and tours, she is making an important contribution to the community. She feels that these actions help strengthen neighborhoods and encourage economic and social growth. Because her plan to create a vacation rental property differed from Feerer's desire to live in the home, Pritzker was able to close the property and complete all the assorted restoration projects at one time. Pritzker has said that she "has a passion for architecture and history; the project never really seemed intimidating but was an enjoyable challenge that was demanding but a lot of fun."

Pritzker's restoration efforts focused on two separate goals: to replicate the home's 1915 appearance, and to develop a first-class property that could be used for vacations and event rentals. Revenue produced by rentals would ensure TAWANI would be able to fund a faithful restoration and cover the cost of proper maintenance to protect the integrity of the home. Restoration would also have the added benefit of respectfully propelling urban change in a positive direction, providing the community with the opportunity to experience a Wright home, and spurring growth and economic progress within the neighborhood. Nationally there are few Frank Lloyd Wright homes that provide accommodation for overnight rental, which only adds to the Bach House's appeal.

The restoration architectural firm that was hired for the project was the Chicago-based company Harboe Architects, established in March 2006 by T. Gunny Harboe.[37] To initiate the second phase of the restoration project, Harboe's firm completed a detailed analysis of the building's exterior and interior. The preliminary investigation focused on fourteen separate areas that required further study. The firm was then able to create a list of concerns and recommendations for the restoration project.

To accomplish much of the restoration work, Harboe Architects consulted with three other companies. Building Conservation Associates was hired to complete analysis on building material and paint finishes, Enspect Engineering consulted on the structural work, and Architectural Consulting Engineers assisted with reviewing the building's service systems, including the mechanical, electrical, and plumbing—or MEP—systems. They also provided consulting services for the ground source heat pump system.

They then provided Pritzker with several options for consideration. To bring the home back to its 1915 appearance, the restoration team worked meticulously to replicate many of the home's exterior features and the original interior wall and ceiling finishes. They also sought to bring back many of Wright's Prairie School elements. To sustain the long-term viability of the building as a vacation property, an option to replace the home's traditional furnace and air conditioning facilities with a ground source heating and cooling system was also offered. One of the contractors that worked on the restoration projects stated, "TAWANI Enterprises wanted to do everything right!"[38]

Two of the major construction projects that were fundamental in bringing the home back to its 1915 appearance were the opening of the second-floor sun porch, which had been roofed in and enclosed for living quarters, and reestablishing the first floor's screened porch, which had been turned into a family room.

The firm of Harboe Architects was able to rehire the same construction manager who had managed the renovations which Jane Feerer had completed when she owned the house, and together they solicited proposals from various companies and tradesmen to complete the second phase of the restoration.

Phase 2 Projects

South patio

The south patio is the raised area bounded by retaining walls to the west, a concrete curb to the south, the garden wall to the east and the house to the north. The walkway and stairs leading to the patio act as the main entrance to the home. The restoration team recreated the original configuration of this space based on the 1915 construction documents.

Courtesy of Building Conservation Associates, Inc.

Courtesy of Building Conservation Associates, Inc.

South patio before restoration

Exterior walls

There are three distinctive exterior wall structures on the property: the retaining walls that create the borders of the south patio; the garden wall that separates the patio from the rear yard space; and the north stair wall, which runs along the sidewalk that leads to the home's rear entry. To restore each of these wall sections, crews deconstructed the walls and salvaged as many of the original bricks as possible. The wooden porthole screen atop the garden wall was removed intact. In each wall section, drainage tiles were installed, and the walls were rebuilt using a combination of salvaged and new brick. New concrete copings were installed on both the patio retaining walls and the northern walkway wall, and the porthole screen on the garden wall was reinstalled.

Courtesy of Harboe Architects

Retaining wall bordering the south patio before restoration

Courtesy of Harboe Architects

Garden wall before restoration

Courtesy of Harboe Architects

North stair wall after restoration

Brickwork and tuckpointing

In some areas salvaged bricks were used to make repairs. However, when necessary, new bricks were installed. Extensive research was completed to match the color and style of the original 1915 bricks with modern-made replacements. As was common in many of Wright's Prairie-style homes, the original specifications stated that the vertical mortar joints were to be struck flush with the adjoining brick to obscure these vertical lines. The horizontal joints were raked out, deepening them to accentuate the horizontal line of the house. All tuckpointing work that was completed during the second phase of restoration was done according to these original specifications.

Courtesy of Building Conservation Associates, Inc.

Matching the original textured brick was challenging, but a suitable match was found.

Concrete base

In some areas, the concrete base of the building and sills had fractured, and these voids had allowed water infiltration and delamination to occur. The restoration team repaired the cracks, and the delaminated areas were removed. Repairs were completed with a concrete mix that matched the color and texture of the original concrete. To ensure the long-term viability of these repairs, a water-repellent sealer was applied to the exterior concrete.

Courtesy of Building Conservation Associates, Inc.

Above: concrete copings during restoration
Below: flat work repairs before restoration

Courtesy of Building Conservation Associates, Inc.

Outer walls

During the investigation and materials analysis of the exterior stucco surfaces, it was discovered that the original exteriors had been overcoated with multiple layers of stucco to complete various repairs that had been required over the years. The stucco had also been painted. However, when the original stucco was uncovered, the team saw that it had an unpainted gray finish. During the restoration, the existing stucco that was found intact was retained. The areas where repairs were needed had new wood furring strips and diamond metal lath installed, and then all the stucco was recovered with new material designed to match the original in color and texture.

Courtesy of Building Conservation Associates, Inc.

Soffit stucco showing various layers of past repairs

Exterior woodwork

The material analysis of the exterior woodwork revealed that the trellises and wood trim had an oil-based, semi-transparent stain that allowed the wood grain to show through. Over time, the stain had been painted over. All the exterior woodwork was stripped down to bare wood, and a new semi-transparent stain that matched the original specifications was applied.

Courtesy of Harboe Architects

Above: Wood trellis system
Below: Landscape plan

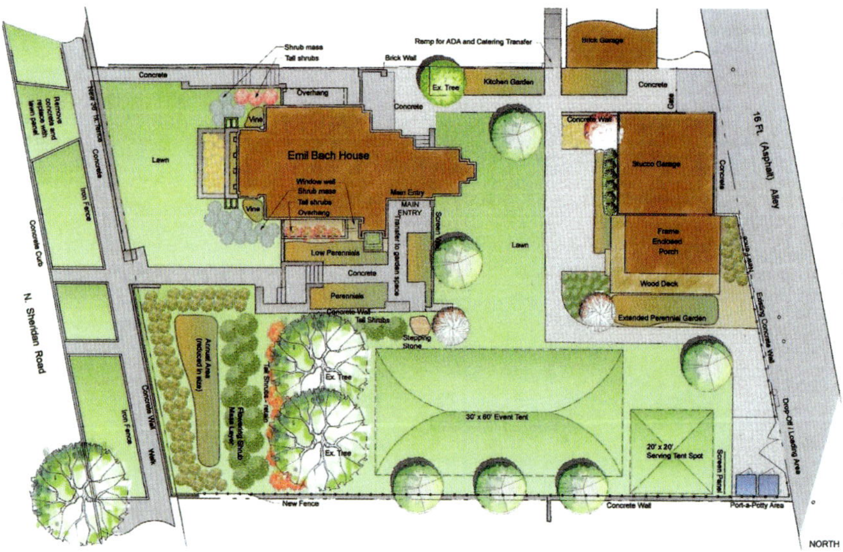

Courtesy of Carol JH Yetken / CYLA Design Associates Inc.

Landscaping plan

Since Frank Lloyd Wright had not created a specific landscaping design in 1915, a new landscape plan was created for the second phase of restoration. The landscape architecture firm of CYLA Design Associates, located in Oak Park, Illinois, was retained to create a conceptual landscaping plan that would incorporate both the home site and the vacant lot to the south.

CYLA Design Associates had worked on as many as twenty Frank Lloyd Wright projects, so they were adept at creating a plan that would enhance the property by showcasing the Bach House as the "jewel of the site." CYLA Design Associates used a natural palette of plant color choices; they wanted to avoid loud colors. They achieved this by selecting several native plants that have adapted to the local climate and have root systems that will thrive in the area's sandy soils.

Plant varieties

Forty-two different plant species were chosen for placement in and around the site. Some of the more popular varieties included smooth sumac, black-eyed Susans, sassafras, and sweet fern. A few black oak trees were planted, along with an assortment of annuals and perennials. Hardscaping on the site included a new paver walkway around the tea house and a new fence around the rear of the property that included a service gate for deliveries. The landscaping on the vacant lot allowed for the use of tents and chair placements, which could be used for weddings and other events.

First-floor porch

The first floor porch was originally an outdoor screened-in porch that was later enclosed by windows. The north-facing entry doors had been removed and the opening filled in with brick masonry. As part of the restoration, and in keeping with the owner's desire to bring the house back to the 1915 appearance, all of these doors and windows were removed. The brickwork that closed off the entryway was removed and a new doorway installed, along with new screens and a new set of French doors leading into the house. These alterations returned the porch to its original open design.

Courtesy of Harboe Architects

Top: plain glass cabinet door
Bottom: Recreated art glass

Courtesy of TAWANI Enterprises

Living room built-in furniture art glass

The bookshelves that face the entry hall originally had an art glass cabinet door covering one section of the shelf system. It was thought that this original Wright designed art piece was lost to time; however, James Blinder informed the restoration team that he still owned this art glass panel. Blinder made the piece available for the project team to duplicate, and this reproduction piece is now installed in the bookcase.

First floor interior ceiling and wall plaster

Previously salvaged fragments of the original interior ceiling plaster and the upper sections of the plaster walls where they joined the ceiling showed that these surfaces were an unpainted material, but the ceiling and the wall sections had been painted at some time in the past. The restoration team covered the existing ceiling plaster and upper wall section with a thin coat of material that matched the aggregate, color, and texture of the original specifications. Because the original ceiling and wall sections were unpainted, this material was left unpainted as well. As part of the first phase of restoration, the lower section of the plaster walls had been reinstalled. During the second phase of the project, the walls were painted with a color that more closely matched Wright's specifications for Sunshine yellow.

First-floor windows

The first-floor casement windows that are currently in the house are believed to be original. The restoration team found that most of these windows had been secured shut, but the original drawings showed that these windows were in fact operable. The restoration of these windows included completing repairs to the sashes and installing new period-specific hardware and screens, and all windows that were originally operable were reconfigured to swing open again.

Dining chairs and buffet table

At the dining room table we find six caned chairs; certainly one doesn't automatically think of Wright creating this style of chair. However, he included caned chairs in two other commissions from around the same time period as the Bach House. Wright designed two different styles of caned chairs for the lobby of the Imperial Hotel in Tokyo, Japan, which opened in 1923 after being constructed from designs that dated back to 1916. The first design included a diamond-back support with caning on the lower side panels, the second design had caned-side panels but also a square caned back. This version also includes pillows for the seat and backrest.

Wright also designed caned chairs for the Sherman Booth House, which was constructed in 1915 and located in the Ravine Bluffs Development in Glencoe, Illinois. The dining room chairs from the Booth House and the dining chairs from the Bach House are almost identical.

The caned chairs Wright designed for the Bachs were on the original building plans and may have been offered to the Bachs as a cost-saving alternative to having Wright design a completely new set of chairs. Their relatively small footprint also works very well to conserve space in the compact dining area.

Courtesy of TAWANI Enterprises

Chicago History Museum

Left: Bach House dining chair. *Right:* Booth House dining chair

Sun porch

The second-floor sun porch was originally an exterior space, so this space was brought back to the original look by removing all post-1915 installations.

Courtesy of Harboe Architects

Enclosed sun porch before restoration

Second-floor bedroom millwork

The original drawings indicated that each of the bedrooms was to have a distinctive piece of built-in furniture. Over time, all these original pieces had been removed. Quality Finishing and Custom Cabinetry was hired again to recreate these signature furniture pieces in the second-floor bedrooms. This company also installed new walnut wood trim and new French doors. To obtain approval from the Landmarks Commission to continue the second phase of restoration, Harboe Architects recreated exact measured drawings of the pieces of furniture, and each piece was then custom-made to these specifications.

One of the biggest challenges of making this custom furniture was dealing with the ongoing effects of temperature and humidity changes in the building. The fit and finish of all the furniture had to be of extremely good quality. All the wood furniture, the French doors, and wood trim are walnut, as originally specified by Wright. The beautiful color of each of these custom-made pieces adds to the drama and boldness of the house's overall design. The walnut wood is sturdy, solid, and shows only a minimal degree of change when exposed to humidity. The wood stands up well under daily use, so it is a good choice for the dining table as well as the dresser, the makeup table, and the doors.

Courtesy of TAWANI Enterprises

Built-in dresser in master bedroom

Courtesy of TAWANI Enterprises

Built-in makeup table in guest room

Second-floor windows

When the second phase of restoration began, it was known that the six second-floor art glass windows had been removed from the building many years ago and that the remaining windows needed repairs similar to the first-floor windows. The six original art glass windows were recreated using an original sample from James Blinder. The remaining windows were repaired and had new glazing, hardware, and interior screens installed.

Courtesy of Harboe Architects

Previous owner James Blinder with an original Bach House art glass window

Courtesy of TAWANI Enterprises

Recreated art glass window

Roofing systems

There are essentially three different roofing systems on the Bach House. The first roofing section is referred to as the lower roof, and it covers the first-floor portions of the house that are not covered by the second floor of the building. Typical of Wright's designs, there are no downspouts or traditional gutter systems on the building. The lower roof sections are pitched so that water will travel to circular openings in the structures and then fall to the ground. The second roof structure is composed of seven individual eyebrow roofs—small, cantilevered roofs—above the bedroom windows, attached to the bottoms of the north and south cantilevered balconies and above the front-facing piers and windows. These eyebrow roofs are angled slightly so that water will drain off of them to the areas below. The upper roof consists of a flat roofing system, and a bird's-eye view of the roof resembles the shape of a Greek cross (illustrated in the photo on page 29). All these roofing systems required repairs and upgrades, and then new bitumen roof coatings were installed on each roof deck.

Bach House roof system before the second floor sun porch was reopened. The upper roof is at the top, and the lower roof skirts the area below the second story windows. Note the eyebrow roof about the leftmost window—the original enclosed portion of the house ended here.

Chimney

The restoration team found that the chimney had been reconfigured over the years and was much smaller than the original. The chimney was rebuilt to conform to current building codes and to a similar size and shape as the original specified by Wright.

Heating and cooling systems

One of the new features in the second-phase restoration plan was the installation of a ground source heat pump system. During the winter, this type of system absorbs heat stored in the ground through underground water pipes that circulate in a loop. The heated water is concentrated and then sent into the building as warm air. During the summer, the cooling system absorbs heat from the building and transfers it into the underground loop system where it is then cooled. The pump uses the cooled water returning from the ground to create cool dehumidified air conditioning. This modern system is efficient and very inexpensive to operate.

Additional furniture

Another modern element to the restoration was the installation of comfortable pieces of furniture and selected pieces of art work. Some pieces of furniture were created specifically for this project, and others were chosen so that they could be used by the people who would attend events at the Bach House or who would stay there as overnight guests. The interior design firm of Morgante-Wilson from Evanston, Illinois, was hired to add furniture and other decorative pieces to the home. Morgante-Wilson's staff used a design scheme that would balance modern accents with Wright's interiors. They were not trying to replicate the 1915 home but rather worked on providing guests with unique pieces of furniture. The pieces selected were placed to augment Wright's designs and create a distinctive atmosphere in each room. Upon entering the home, we are met with a beautiful Chinese stone from the Pagoda Red Stone Company. The piece is mounted on a wood-and-Plexiglas stand and is seen from both the entryway and the inglenook. The polished surface is tranquil and evokes the flow of water from the nearby lake.

Courtesy of TAWANI Enterprises

Chinese stone

Leaving the entryway and traveling towards the inglenook we encounter more distinctive pieces installed in the home including a Ruché sofa, designed in 2010, and a modern barrel lamp from Crate & Barrel.

Courtesy of TAWANI Enterprises

Barrel lamp and blue Ruché sofa

The inglenook includes a large ottoman, which was designed by Morgante-Wilson specifically for this design project. The grayish off-white color of the fabric blends with the brick and mortar chimney and the concrete lintel. The ottoman would be a comfortable spot to sit and warm yourself by the fire or chat with family or friends in the inglenook.

Courtesy of TAWANI Enterprises

Ottoman in inglenook

In the living room we discover a charming table designed by Osvaldo Borsani from the 1950s. This piece adds a bit of rolling art work to the room and can be positioned easily anywhere in the room for serving drinks or hors d'oeuvres. Imagine an intimate dinner setting for newlyweds or a party of four enjoying a casual dining experience.

Courtesy of TAWANI Enterprises

Borsani table

In the corner of the living room is a modern Anda chair and ottoman designed by Pierre Paulin from 2009 that engulfs your body in stylishness. The curved seat and swooping arms support you in comfort, and the ottoman acts as an extension of the chair for your weary legs to rest upon.

Courtesy of TAWANI Enterprises

Courtesy of TAWANI Enterprises

Top: Anda chair. *Bottom:* Utrecht chair

A beautiful Utrecht armchair designed by Gerrit T. Rietveld in 1935 was added to the guest bedroom. Rietveld lived in the Netherlands from 1888 to 1964, and he designed modernistic furniture. For a time, Rietveld was a leading figure in the De Stijl movement, which utilized horizontal and vertical lines as well as black, white, and primary colors, and flourished in Europe from 1917 until 1931. This chair creates an interesting link between Frank Lloyd Wright and the De Stijl designers whose proponents were followers of Cubist theories. Wright was not a Cubist architect, but his designs for breaking the box evoke a similar expression.

A classically designed 1999 mid-century Case Study daybed by Modernica was used in the children's bedroom. The daybed can be used by vacationers for lounging and relaxing after a day of Chicago sightseeing or as an extra sleeping space for the weary traveler. The child's room also includes a Noir Furniture three-ball pedestal table. This table can be used for any number of purposes and also stands alone as another piece of purposeful artwork.

One piece of functional art that predates the work completed by Morgante-Wilson is the Sourlis glass lamp that sits atop the walnut mantel of the chimney extension that is centered in the dining table.

Courtesy of TAWANI Enterprises

Sourlis lamp

The lamp was commissioned by Jane Feerer, who wanted a piece that would be unique. The piece she chose is a custom manufactured lamp from the Sourlis Glass Studio located in Highland, Indiana. Not unlike Frank Lloyd Wright, the makers of this custom piece use nature for their inspiration. Using distinctive pieces of glass manufactured by the Uroboros Glass Company in Portland, Oregon, and custom metal fins to join these one-of-a-kind glass creations, Sourlis Glass Studio had created the unique item Feerer was looking for. Feerer felt that the lamp so embodied the spirit of the house it should be kept in its original location, so she decided to include the lamp in the sale of the home.

The modern furniture, the artwork, and the recreated chairs, tables, and other pieces of built-in furniture designed by Wright combine to bring a comfortable but elegant feel to each living space. The two phases of the restoration took a building that was almost 100 years old and had been the home to ten different families—who all had in some way left their mark on the home—and turned it into a revitalized and timeless work of art.

CHAPTER TWELVE
The Bach House Today

TODAY, THE BACH HOUSE SERVES the Chicago community in multiple ways. It stands as the work of art Wright designed it to be but also opens its spaces to visitors for uses that only add to its charm.

A Vacation Rental

Frank Lloyd Wright's Emil Bach House is one of the beautifully restored properties managed by TAWANI Stone Heritage, and it is the only Wright home in Chicago that is available as a vacation rental.

When renting the house all of the facilities of the home are included, so guests can personally experience the joys of "living" in a Frank Lloyd Wright home today. The Japanese tea house, the sun porch, and the outdoor grounds are included in each rental.

Typical hotel amenities such as soaps, shampoo, conditioner, and luxurious linens are included, and there are cozy cotton bathrobes available for each guest. An indoor parking space is also available for a minimal fee. A small kiosk displays an assortment of inspired gifts and souvenirs, which are available for purchase.

The Bach House has consistently received high ratings from those who have toured the home, held an event there, or stayed for a vacation. On the Bach House Facebook page, visitor Kevin Frost said the house was an "absolutely stunning example of Wright architecture including Japanese elements, a secluded secret entryway, and more." TripAdvisor reviewer Zachary L. stated, "I had a fantastic weekend with family and friends at the Emil Bach House. The house was both artistically fascinating and equipped with every amenity I could ask for."

A Place to Gather

The house is available for couples and their families to host weddings, civil unions, holiday parties, or any other family celebration. The site, which includes the home, tea house, and gardens, can hold up to 125 guests for many types of catered events. The complex may also be used by businesses for meetings, team-building programs, or other corporate affairs.

Courtesy of TAWANI Enterprises

Families can gather at the Bach House to celebrate marriage

Tracy Smigielski said of the Bach House in a Yelp review, "When we got engaged, we knew immediately we wanted to have our wedding reception at the Bach House, because the house is absolutely beautiful. We didn't even need to do much in the way of decorating; we let the house speak for itself, we were all truly impressed by the amazing details of the house, both inside and out."

The Frank Lloyd Wright Trust has hosted several "After Hours" programs at the Bach House. These evening events allow visitors to experience a Wright house in a casual, festive atmosphere. The events, which are modestly priced, include light hors d'oeuvres, drinks, and music. Tour guides on site provide information to guests and act as ambassadors for the Frank Lloyd Wright Trust.

Courtesy of TAWANI Enterprises

Above: The tea house is a lovely setting for wedding photographs
Below: an "After Hours" event at the Bach House

Courtesy of TAWANI Enterprises

An Enchanting Tour

For daily visitors, tours of the building and grounds are currently being offered by the Frank Lloyd Wright Trust from May through September. The Trust volunteers conduct these visits in a relaxed environment and focus on Frank Lloyd Wright, original owners Emil and Anna Bach, and the restoration. Typically, the tours are conducted for small groups of devoted Wright aficionados or for individuals who enjoy touring historic homes. The average number of guests range between thirty to thirty-five people per week. Longtime Trust volunteer Bill Kundert elaborated on responses he has received from guests following Bach House tours he has given: "Responses are uniformly positive. I think the most common reaction expressed is that they love the house and they could imagine living here. I think many of the guests are surprised that Wright designed for, and was concerned for, the person of more average means looking for an affordable house."

Courtesy of TAWANI Enterprises

Bach House guide Bill Kundert leads visitors on a tour

Indeed, Jimmy Lew stated on Yelp that he loved how the home "is privately owned by an individual for short term rental, so it was different and interesting to see how one might go about restoring the interior in the best way possible."

Another Yelper, Sarah Simons, said, “Thanks to Open House Chicago I was able to experience the Emil Bach House; it was a once in a lifetime experience for me.”

Courtesy of TAWANI Enterprises

A selection of gifts available from the Bach House

EPILOGUE

ONCE A BUILDING IS CONSTRUCTED and the owners move in, they begin to make their house a home. Owners will bring in their own furniture, may change the color of the walls, and will make changes in the landscaping, all in an effort to create their own special household. Each owner has the right to create his or her vision of a home to be loved and cherished regardless of who the architect was, even if that architect was Frank Lloyd Wright. However, the opposite can also be true: if the owner longs for the magical experience of living in a Wright-designed home, then they will spare no expense to build, restore, and preserve their Wright home.

The Bachs and the other early owners of the house have passed away. As of the writing of this book, former owners James Blinder, Sirirat Banuchi, and Reza Toulabi were still living and working in the Chicago area.

Jane Feerer, who owned the home from 2005 to 2011, has moved out of the Chicago area but is involved in financial consulting, and she is a clergy member in the Episcopal Church. And Jennifer Pritzker, the current owner of the Bach House, is an investor, philanthropist, and retired lieutenant colonel of the United States Army.

These owners placed distinctive stamps on the house:

- The Bachs carried through on Frank Lloyd Wright's design and built the home.
- Either the Spiesmans or the Weiss family enclosed the sun porch.
- James Blinder began some initial renovations that protected the integrity of the building by replacing the roof and boiler, and he rewired the

electrical system. He renovated the kitchen, bathroom, and basement and converted the maid's second floor bedroom into a second bathroom.

- Miller sought out landmark status for the building, and the Banuchis donated the preservation easement on the home, likely saving it from demolition.
- Jane Feerer and Jennifer Pritzker both contributed to completing the extensive and period-specific restoration of the building.

The Significance of the House's Transitional Design

At first glance, one might not see in the Bach House the grand Prairie-style attributes found in many of Wright's early Prairie homes, but by visiting or living in the house one will experience walking up the path of discovery to find a petite garden space juxtaposed with the main entry. From early in his career, Wright shunned the boxy look of the typical Victorian home. To avoid creating a house that looks like one box on top of another, he incorporated a series of trellises and clean, simple lines into the cantilevered balconies to lighten the building's look. These balconies and trellises were Wright's way of breaking up the cube-like look of the house.

The protective overhanging eaves of the flat cross axial roof gives the dweller a sense of security and protection. After walking through the main door, in almost every room the explorer will find hints of Japanese architecture that Wright uses to beautify the living spaces. The brick structured chimney, the walnut woodwork, and the stylized art glass windows that Wright employed allowed him to use art and architecture to create an indoor universe that is as serene as it is beautiful. With the home's unobstructed view of Lake Michigan in 1915, Wright tried to provide the homeowner with two tranquil outdoor spaces from which to experience nature: the lower screened porch would have been shaded and cool, and the second-floor balcony provided the seated guest with an outstanding view. Even today, these two areas provide the home's occupants a place to rest and relax away from the busy traffic-filled street and experience a dynamic view of the grounds.

Frank Lloyd Wright's residential architecture can be loosely grouped into four general areas:

- Pre-Prairie designs, 1889–1900
- Prairie designs, 1900–1915
- Manufactured projects, 1913–1924
- Usonian, 1937–1959

The Bach House was designed at the end of Wright's Prairie period and is considered a transitional design because, like some of the home designs that immediately pre-date the house and those that came shortly afterward, it was designed for an American family living on a modest budget. Wright's homes from the Ravine Bluffs development, his American System-Built Homes, and his California textile block houses from 1923—which could be constructed by a contractor or possibly, with some "sweat equity," the homeowners themselves—share similar attributes for budget-minded home buyers. The homes were designed to be compact, sturdy, durable, and—most importantly to Frank Lloyd Wright—beautiful. All these attributes can be found in the Bach House.

The home's link to Wright's Usonian designs is visible in the living spaces that flow seamlessly one into the other, a characteristic common to that style. Usonian bedrooms are small but comfortably sized, while the family's living spaces are larger and designed to be shared. The home's bedrooms on the second floor offer a quiet rest area, but they are not designed as rooms to be lived in. The Usonian will effortlessly blend with nature; the Bach House's gardens, screened porch, and sun porch are all attributes that precede the Usonian's natural connection.

The Restoration

By completing a historically accurate restoration, Jennifer Pritzker has established the Bach House as a premier destination for visitors to the Rogers Park neighborhood of Chicago. The house's dedicated owners have understood that preservation of a historic building inspires visitors to learn about the past and how that past influences our future. They have also offered the community at large a long-lasting cultural asset. The building provides a sense of identity to the area and helps explain how Rogers Park was founded and grew in the early twentieth century. Having a Chicago landmark in the heart of Rogers Park gives residents of the neighborhood a touchstone to the past.

Knowing that there is a prestigious Chicago landmark in their own neighborhood gives residents the encouragement to maintain or rehabilitate their own homes. By promoting historic preservation, grassroots organizations may seek other homes in the neighborhood that have architecturally significant features or that are historically important and work toward rehabilitating them as well. All the preservation efforts help create a stimulating and energetic neighborhood with improved property values where tourism contributes to a growth in traffic for local business owners. The events and tours that take place at the home are open to all members of society, and these community events bring neighbors and family members together where they can share the loveliness of the home along with their own stories.

If you have explored the Bach House, you can continue this experience of history and beauty in various ways. If you are a visitor from out of town, maybe you will be inspired to seek out a building in your city that is historically significant and begin efforts to restore that property. Or maybe you are an intrepid Frank Lloyd Wright building explorer who has added another tour site to an ever-growing list of visits. You may even be a local visitor who will become inspired to become a volunteer tour guide for the Frank Lloyd Wright Trust. All these are possibilities now that you've have been inspired by this late prairie home.

You may also want to expand your own research into Frank Lloyd Wright. There are as many as 1,100 building designs detailed in the three-volume set *Frank Lloyd Wright: Complete Works* by Bruce Brooks Pfeiffer and Peter Gossel. Volume 1 covers the years 1885–1916, Volume 2 discusses the years 1917–1942, and Volume 3 completes the set with the years 1943–1959. You can focus your research on Wright's interest in Japanese art prints, the Froebel blocks, or nature. You can also research how Wright's work influenced other architects, artists, and designers in the United States, Europe, and Japan. You'll likely find that Wright's influence is far-reaching and has many different nuances to be explored.

When visiting the Bach House, you feel a different sense of time and place. The home is simultaneously old and new; it is an American Prairie-style building influenced by traditional Japanese art and architecture. Though built in a metropolitan area, it has a pastoral feel with its wide lot, flowered gardens, and its closeness to Lake Michigan.

When you are in the home, you experience Wright's ability to create spaces without walls as you move through the first floor. The second floor bedrooms boast their beautiful art glass windows, and private balconies provide you with the feeling of peace and serenity. The outdoor spaces are quiet and still, like a peaceful oasis from the busy, modern world.

Our goal is to share this charming building with you and to provide each guest with a unique experience that will bring you back again.

The story of the Emil Bach House began in 1915, and, with ongoing stewardship from TAWANI Enterprises, the building will still be here in the year 2115 and beyond for many more to enjoy.

By reading this book, you have become part of the community that admires and supports the Emil Bach House. Use these pages to add your own experiences and memories to the Bach House's continuing story, linking the past to the future.

APPENDIX

Ruth Bach's Recollections of Meeting Frank Lloyd Wright

The *American Institute of Architects Journal* published a story written by Ruth Bach, Theodore Bach's wife, in the October 1972 issue. The story, titled "It Happened Only Once," was printed on page 65 in the "letters" section and details how Ruth Bach met Frank Lloyd Wright around 1932. The text of the published letter and the story included here are slightly different; it's possible the editor took some liberties to shorten the story to meet the length quota he must have been working with.

The entire letter as typed out (likely by Ruth Bach herself) is reprinted here.

towns they have to be given thought and created simultaneously.

To illustrate the diversity of subjects of interest which required attention in day to day association, I mention museum planning which came upon the horizon via the Wichita Art Museum. Realizing that light is necessary to see, we were convinced that museums should be planned, among other basics, for the best circumstances under which one sees what is being exhibited. So we studied museum lighting and published an article on the subject in the *Architectural Forum*. Soon thereafter, the International Institute of Intellectual Cooperation of the League of Nations in 1934 decided to hold an international conference on the study of architecture and the planning of art museums. Presumably on the strength of the above mentioned article, Stein was invited to deliver a paper on museum lighting.

Stein is one of the few architects to have received the highest honor of recognition from the AIA—its Gold Medal.

ISADORE ROSENFIELD, FAIA
New York, N.Y.

It Happened Only Once

There are really only a few distinctions to which I can lay claim, but there is one which surpasses all the others. I probably am the only living soul who ever actually slammed the door in the face of Frank Lloyd Wright.

As I look back upon the incident, almost 40 years later, I find it highly amusing. But at the time, since I was a young bride trying to make a good impression on my husband's family, it seemed catastrophic.

My husband's mother, who is now 90 years old, was a woman with a passion for the practical and functional in living. When she decided to build a home and began to consult architects, she decided that Frank Lloyd Wright was the only one who could combine these two characteristics and add the beauty necessary to create the type of home she desired. So together they designed the house in which my husband was raised and into which, shortly after our marriage, we moved.

At the time of the "incident," my mother-in-law was already becoming an arthritic cripple and was finding it quite difficult to cope with the stairs. However, most afternoons she would slowly make her way to take a long rest, leaving me to "hold the fort" below. These were days of the Depression and myriads of people seemed to be selling door-to-door merchandise, and we were constantly annoyed by the ringing doorbell. Mother was a pushover for these unfortunates and seldom turned them down if they had anything salable that she could possibly use. I, being young with much less purchasing power, was inclined to be less charitable.

On the particular afternoon of my great goof, Mother had just painfully made her way upstairs and probably was just settling for a nap. I was in the midst of a sewing storm. I say "storm" because I so thoroughly loathed the sight of a needle.

When the doorbell chimed, I was in no hurry to investigate, but I did get eventually to the glassed reception hall. What I saw did not impress me favorably: a middle-aged, nondescript looking man wearing a sadly battered hat, waiting patiently.

Cautiously I opened the door, and he asked politely if he could see Mrs. Bach. Since he knew the correct name, I hesitated briefly and then said that I would see if she could come. Slamming the door, I left him standing, hat in hand, while I went to confer with Mother.

She decided that since the man had asked for her personally she had better come and investigate. I helped her as much as possible, knowing that a great deal of time was elapsing. Imagine my horror when the minute she glimpsed him she let out a gasp, "Why, it's Mr. Wright! Let him in!" All of a sudden I realized that it was Wright, the famous architect. I made quick steps to admit him.

He was most gracious. He inquired about my mother-in-law's health and proceeded to discuss various features of the house with her. It seems that he had the habit of returning frequently to his houses to review ideas in this manner.

The two of them had a lively discussion and enjoyed their visit. I stayed in the background, needless to say, until the end of his call when he turned to me and said, "So this is your new daughter-in-law!" and that was all. There was nothing more to say.

MRS. RUTH BACH
Rockford, Ill.

Ruth Bach's letter in the *American Institute of Architects Journal*, October 1972

(1) Ruth Bach

Courtesy of Owen Bach family

IT HAPPENED ONLY ONCE

There are really only a few distinctions to which I can lay claim but there is one which I believe surpasses all the others. I think I am probably the only living soul who ever actually slammed the door in the face of Frank Lloyd Wright.

As I look back over the incident, almost forty years later, I find it highly amusing. But at the time it occurred, since I was a young bride trying to make a good impression on my husband's family, it seemed catastrophic.

My husband's mother, who is now ninety years old and a complete invalid in a California nursing home, was a woman with a passion for the practical and functional in living. When she decided to build a home and began to consult architects she decided that Frank Lloyd Wright was the only one who could combine these two characteristics and add the beauty necessary to create the type of home she desired. So together they designed the house in which my husband was raised and into which, shortly after our marriage, we moved. I suppose it might be considered somewhat of a distinction, and certainly a privilege, to have lived in the house - it was so comfortable and beautiful.

At the time of "the incident" my mother-in-law was already becoming an arthritic cripple and was finding it quite difficult to cope with the stairs. However, most afternoons she would slowly make her way up to take a long rest leaving me to "hold the fort" below. Since these were depression days and myriads of people seemed to be selling door-to-door merchandise we were constantly being annoyed by the ringing door-bell. Mother was a

(2)

"[illegible] over" for these unfortunates and seldom turned them [illegible] if [illegible] anything saleable she could [illegible]. [illegible] with much less purchasing power, was inclined to be less charitable.

On the particular afternoon of my "great goof" mother had just painfully made her way upstairs and I imagine was just comfortably settled down for a nap. I was in the midst of a sewing storm - I say storm because I so thoroughly loathed the sight of a needle - and probably not in the best of humor. So when the door-bell chimed I was in no hurry to investigate, but did eventually get to the glassed reception hall. What I saw did not impress me favorably - a middle-aged, nondescript looking man wearing a sadly battered hat, patiently waiting. I realized he had seen me so decided it was necessary at least to open the door to find out what he was selling since there was no evidence of the usual case of notions or brushes.

I opened the door somewhat cautiously (although these were not very dangerous times, even in Chicago) and in a low, pleasant voice he asked very politely if he could see Mrs. B. Since he knew the correct name I hesitated briefly, then said I would see if she could come, and slamming the door left him standing, hat in hand by this time, while I went to confer with mother. She decided that since he had asked for her personally she had better come down and investigate. I helped her as much as possible knowing that a great deal of time was elapsing. Imagine my horror when the minute she could glimpse through the glass she let out a gasp, "Why, it's Mr. Wright! Let him in!" For an instant this didn't impress me greatly but all of a sudden I realized it was Frank Lloyd Wright, the famous architect. I made quick steps to admit him, you may be sure, apologizing as best I could. He was most gracious. He inquired about mother's health and proceeded

Courtesy of Owen Bach family

(3)

to discuss various features of the house with her. It seems he had a habit of returning frequently to his houses to review ideas in this manner, and I think he enjoyed mother's practical philosophy.

The two of them had a lively discussion and enjoyed their visit. I stayed in the background, needless to say, until the end of his call when he turned to me and said, "So this is your new daughter-in-law!" and that was all. There was nothing more to say.

Courtesy of Owen Bach family

GLOSSARY

English words

Alcove	A recess in the wall of a room or garden
Armoire	A wardrobe or movable cabinet, typically one that is ornate
Arts and Crafts movement	A social and artistic movement of the second half of the 19th century emphasizing a return to handwork, skilled craftsmanship, and attention to design in the decorative arts
Belvedere	An architectural structure built in an elevated position to provide lighting and ventilation and commands a view.
Caned chair	A chair with a seat (and sometimes a back) that is made of woven cane, often rattan, and similar to wickerwork
Cantilever	A rigid structural element projecting from a vertical support
Casement window	A window that swings out on hinges that are generally attached to the upright side of its frame
Coping	A finishing or protective course or cap to an exterior masonry wall

Cross-axial	A building or structure arranged lengthwise, along a given axis.
Cubism	A style of painting or sculpture developed in the early 20th century that reduced natural forms to their geometric equivalents
Diamond metal lath	Metal material with diamond-shaped mesh that is commonly used to support plaster or stucco
Eave	The part of a roof that meets or overhangs the walls of a building
Eyebrow window	A small roof projecting from the slope of a building's main roof, often over a window
Façade	The face of a building, especially the principal front that looks onto a street or open space
French door	A door with glass panes throughout its length
Froebel blocks	Wooden play materials for young children designed by Friedrich Froebel
Ground source heat pump system	A central heating and/or cooling system that transfers heat to or from the ground
Hardscaping	Man-made features used in landscape architecture such as paths or walls, as contrasted with vegetation
Hip roof	A hip roof, hip-roof, or hipped roof is a type of roof where all sides slope downwards to the walls, usually with a fairly gentle slope.
Inglenook	A nook by a fireplace including a bench or settle

Japanese wood-block printing	A printing technique best known for its use in ukiyo-e art, especially during the Edo period (1603-1868). It was also used for printing books in the same period.
Millwork	Any type of woodwork that is produced in a mill such as doors, molding, trim, flooring, wall paneling and crown molding.
Ottoman	An upholstered, often overstuffed seat or couch, usually without a back.
Pergola	An archway consisting of a framework often covered with trained climbing or trailing plants.
Pillar	Upright structure of concrete, stone, or brick that support a superstructure or are used for ornamentation.
Polygon	A plane figure with at least three straight sides and angles, and typically five or more.
Porch	A covered shelter projecting in front of the entrance of a building.
Prairie School	An American style of architecture marked by horizontal lines, flat or hip roofs with broad overhanging eaves, and integrated with the surrounding landscape.
Preservation easement	A legal agreement between a property owner and a qualified organization that has the authority to approve or deny any changes to the property.
Ravine Bluffs Development	Frank Lloyd Wright's first built subdivision in the Village of Glencoe, Illinois.

Rhombus A parallelogram with opposite equal acute angles, opposite equal obtuse angles, and four equal sides.

Sash window A window which consists of two frames placed one above the other.

Stucco A fine plaster used for coating wall surfaces or molding into architectural decorations.

Taliesin Meaning "shining brow," it was the name of a 6th-century Welsh poet and the name of Frank Lloyd Wright's home, studio, and school in Spring Green, Wisconsin.

Terrace A level paved area or platform next to a building, a patio, or veranda.

Transom A strengthening crossbar, in particular one set above a window or door.

Trellis A framework of light wooden or metal bars, chiefly used as a support for fruit trees or climbing plants.

Usonian Relating to or denoting the style of buildings designed in the 1930s by Frank Lloyd Wright, characterized by inexpensive construction and flat roofs.

Veranda A roofed platform along the outside of a house, level with the ground floor.

Vertical pier An upright support for a structure such as an arch or bridge, or a section of structural walls between openings.

Victorian architecture The style of architecture popular during the reign of England's Queen Victoria (1837–1901). A typical Victorian home would have a large, wraparound porch with decorative railings. The exterior of the building would be very decorative, and include gabled roofs. There may be a tower at one corner of the building. The interiors would be very ornate, with chandeliers, heavy drapes and large wooded elements.

Water table A masonry feature that projects at the base of a wall to deflect water running down a building away from the foundation.

Wood furring strips A furring strip is a long, thin strip that is typically used to level a surface in order to finish it with stucco or drywall

Japanese words

Chashitsu An architectural space designed to be used for tea ceremony

Engawa A veranda or porch-like space serving as passageway and sitting space

Genkan A bi-level entryway

Hashirakake Japanese art print designed to be hung from a pillar

Ho-o-den A Japanese-style structure created for the 1893 World's Fair in Chicago. It was constructed using traditional methods and its design was based on the Ho-o-Do in Japan.

Irikawa A corridor-like space on the periphery of a room

Jodannoma	A raised floor
Kamoi	A timber slat or trim piece that spans a room
Kirikomihagi	A style of wall in which stones are fitted tightly together
Ramma	A wooden screen for ventilation
Tamagaki	A fence around a temple or home
Ukiyo-e style drawing	A uniquely Japanese art from developed to show scenes of everyday life
Yagura	A tower or turret found on a Japanese castle

Endnotes

1 "How Chicago Got Its Name" by Emily Upton, *Today I Found Out*, accessed July 25, 2015, http://www.todayifoundout.com/index.php/2013/07/how-chicago-got-its-name/.

2 H. Allen Brooks, *The Prairie School: Frank Lloyd Wright and His Contemporaries* (New York: Norton and Company, 1972).

3 Paul Goldberger, "ARCHITECTURE VIEW; Wright Seen Anew as an Architect of Thoughts," *The New York Times*, February 7, 1988, https://www.nytimes.com/1988/02/07/arts/architecture-view-wright-seen-anew-as-an-architect-of-thoughts.html?pagewanted=all.

4 "Wingspread: Frank Lloyd Wright's Largest Prairie-Style House was Home to the Johnsons," SC Johnson, accessed January 11, 2019, https://www.scjohnson.com/A%20Family%20Company/Architecture%20and%20Tours/Frank%20Lloyd%20Wright/Wingspread%20Frank%20Lloyd%20Wrights%20Largest%20Prairie%20Style%20House%20was%20Home%20to%20the%20Johnsons.

5 "Oscar Steffens House: The 'Other' Bach House," by Hank Morris, Rogers Park/West Ridge Historical Society, accessed October 24, 2012, http://rpwrhs.org/w/index.php?title=Oscar_Steffens_House

6 Meryle Secrest, *Frank Lloyd Wright: A Biography* (Chicago: University of Chicago Press, 1992).

7 ibid.

8 William R. Drennan, *Death in a Prairie House: Frank Lloyd Wright and the Taliesin Murders* (Madison, Wisconsin: University of Wisconsin Press, 2007).

9 ibid.

10 Meryle Secrest, *Frank Lloyd Wright: A Biography* (Chicago: University of Chicago Press, 1992).

11 H. Allen Brooks, *The Prairie School: Frank Lloyd Wright and His Contemporaries* (New York: Norton and Company, 1972).

12 United States Census Bureau, *Thirteenth Census of the United States, 1910* (NARA microfilm publication T624, 1,178 rolls). Records of the Bureau of the Census, Record Group 29. National Archives, Washington, DC, accessed at ancestry.com.

13 Paul Kruty, *Frank Lloyd Wright and Midway Gardens* (Urbana, Chicago: University of Illinois Press, 1998).

14 “The Life of American Workers in 1915,” United States Bureau of Labor Statistics, accessed February 1, 2018, https://www.bls.gov/opub/mlr/2016/article/the-life-of-american-workers-in-1915.htm.

15 “Illinois Building Notes,” *The American Contractor*, January 22, 1916, page 35.

16 “Building News,” *The Economist: A Weekly Financial, Commercial, and Real-estate Newspaper*, November 12, 1921, page 1068.

17 “Water table,” Dictionary.com, accessed April 3, 2019, http://www.dictionary.com/browse/water-table.

18 Brent Coleman, “For owner, Wright House was like a family member,” *USA Today*, February 8, 2013, https://www.usatoday.com/story/news/nation/2013/02/08/wright-tonkens-house-side/1903739/.

19 Ulrich Conrads, ed., Michael Bullock, trans., *Programs and Manifestoes on 20th-Century Architecture* (Cambridge, Massachusetts: The MIT Press, 1971).

20 Owen Bach, in discussion with the author, January 21, 2016, March 2, 2016.

21 ibid.

22 Meryle Secrest, *Frank Lloyd Wright: A Biography* (Chicago: University of Chicago Press, 1992).

23 “Frank Lloyd Wright Credited Japan for his All-American Aesthetic” by Kevin Nute, Smithsonian.com, accessed January 20, 2018, https://www.smithsonianmag.com/arts-culture/frank-lloyd-wrights-japanese-education-180963617.

24 Kevin Nute, *Frank Lloyd Wright and Japan* (New York: Van Nostrand Reinhold, 1993).

25 ibid.

26 Melanie Birk, Frank Lloyd Wright Home and Studio Foundation eds., *Frank Lloyd Wright's Fifty Views of Japan: The 1905 Photo Album* (Portland, Oregon: Pomegranate Communications, 1996).

27 Frank Lloyd Wright, *An Autobiography* (London, New York: Longmans, Green & Co., 1932).

28 Leila Edwards and William Kundert, *The Emil Bach House* (Oak Park: Frank Lloyd Wright Preservation Trust, 2013).

29 James Blinder, in discussion with the author, December 14, 2016.

30 Paul Gapp, “Home by Wright: Sincerity is Price,” *The Chicago Tribune*, November 15, 1975.

31 Richard Curtis, “The Wright price: In an unusual move, an original Clifton home goes up for auction,” *Cincinnati Business Courier*, May 12, 2003, https://www.bizjournals.com/cincinnati/stories/2003/05/12/story2.html.

32 “One of Country’s first Frank Lloyd Wright Home Auctions Set for March in Chicago,” *Business Wire*, accessed February 22, 2005, https://www.businesswire.com/news/home/20050222005818/en/Countrys-Frank-Lloyd-Wright-Home-Auctions-Set.

33 Jane Feerer, in discussion with the author, April 16, 2016.

34 “Chicago Landmarks,” City of Chicago, accessed April 3, 2019, https://webapps1.cityofchicago.org/landmarksweb/web/listings.htm.

35 “Illinois Strives to Preserve its Landmarks,” *Harvey Star Tribune*, December 14, 1972.

36 Andrew Schroedter, “Pritzker deal | Lincoln Park listing | Palmolive buyer,” *Crain’s Chicago Business*, December 2, 2010, https://www.chicagobusiness.com/article/20101202/CRED0701/101209976/pritzker-deal-lincoln-park-listing-palmolive-buyer.

37 “About,” Harboe Architects, accessed January 12, 2018, https://www.harboearch.com/about.html.

38 Carol JH Yetken, in discussion with the author, January 30, 2018.

About the Author

An avid admirer of Frank Lloyd Wright's work, Robert Hartnett has volunteered with the Frank Lloyd Wright Trust as a multi-site tour guide in Chicago and Oak Park, Illinois. This book grew out of his belief that the role of architecture in our communities, and the history of the Bach House in particular, are important topics that should be shared in engaging and informative ways. In addition to architectural writing, Bob is a gardener and craftsman. He lives in Illinois with his wife and family.